IRMA and ARTHUR MYERS

Why You Feel Down— & What You Can Do About It

Charles Scribner's Sons / New York

Our thanks to Gordon Northrup, M.D., child psychiatrist, who read this manuscript with care and creativity and made invaluable suggestions.

Copyright © 1982 Irma and Arthur Myers

Library of Congress Cataloging in Publication Data
Myers, Irma.
Why you feel down—& what you can do about it.
Includes index.
1. Depression in children. 2. Adolescent psychology.
I. Myers, Arthur, 1917–   . II. Title. III. Title:
Why you feel down—and what you can do about it.
RJ506.D4M93   616.85′27′0088055   82-3271
ISBN 0-684-17442-1   AACR2

5 7 9 11 13 15 17 19 F/C 20 18 16 14 12 10 8 6 4

Printed in the United States of America

To Tarin Ashley Patrick,
our grandson,
who just turned seven,
five years away from
those adolescent years.

Contents

1/It Goes with the Territory

Amy was the most popular girl in the high school. She was never without a boyfriend. She dressed well, was always out with the crowd, got good marks. Her parents thought of her as the ideal daughter. In fact, everyone thought Amy had it made. If I could only be like Amy, girls thought. But if they'd known how Amy felt, they wouldn't have wanted to be like her. Amy was depressed.

Bill was one of the school's star athletes. He made letters in football, basketball, baseball. He was active in school politics, never failing to hold some office. The girls loved him, and his social life was superactive. People wondered how he had time to do all the things he did. Bill felt he had to do these things. He had to keep running. If he didn't run madly, he felt, boredom—or something worse—would catch up with him. He was right: it would have—because underneath his happy-go-lucky front, Bill was depressed.

1

Miriam got some of the best marks in school, but none of the kids envied her. She spent hours every evening studying because she found it hard to concentrate and had to go over the same pages time after time. And still her marks were slipping. Although she was not bad looking, Miriam never had a boyfriend, almost never went out. She seemed uninterested in social contact. She felt different, alienated, isolated from people, withdrawn into a gray world of her own. She too was depressed.

Fred was the kind of kid who provided a great example —of what not to do. He ran with a tough gang. They drank early and often, were into pot and, some said, heavier stuff. He had twice been hauled into juvenile court, once for vandalism, another time for assault. It was rumored that he had ripped off a few grocery stores and gas stations. At fourteen he had run away from home and been picked up by the cops hitchhiking a hundred miles away. At fifteen, he was waiting impatiently to be sixteen, so he could quit school. And that, thought many teachers, parents, and kids, would be a relief for all concerned—for Fred was the classic bad kid. Actually, his problem was that he was depressed.

Amy, Bill, Miriam, and Fred are not isolated cases. Many adolescents have a generous degree of depression. It often goes with the territory, with this stage of life. The depression may be obvious or subtle. You can't tell whether someone is depressed simply by the way he or she relates to the world. Things are often not what they seem. In fact, adolescents are experts at hiding their real emotions, hiding how they feel inside when they're alone.

Some kids like Amy and Bill—the most popular girl, the star athlete—may not be at all depressed. They may be what they seem: successes in their high school world. But young people like this are not running; they are able to be alone and enjoy their own company. They like themselves. They are not masking depressed feelings.

Teenagers, no matter how they really feel, are often told by adults that this is the happiest time of their lives. It is a rare adult who at one time or another has not expressed this rather envious comment. If this is the happiest time, most harassed kids secretly think, how am I going to feel later? Just because I have my physical comforts taken care of, because I have food, shelter, and can use the family car, doesn't mean that I don't have problems, that I can't feel lousy, that life can't seem a bummer. External comforts don't by any means rule out stress and conflict.

An adolescent is treading a mine field between childhood and adulthood, and there is no map of the battlefield to tell him where to step. Adolescence is a sort of bridge; the individual is moving from the country of childhood to the country of adulthood. And he is leaving behind some things that he misses acutely—his cuteness, his unconditional acceptance by the adult world. He has lost the comfortable, love-filled world of childhood. Now he is *responsible* for the reactions of others to him. This is new, and it can be a real mindbender.

And because the person hasn't traveled this way before, it's hard for him to believe that he is heading for safer territory, once he gets by this specially difficult stretch in life's journey. Things can seem mighty hopeless, and a kid can feel devastatingly helpless.

Adolescents are reaching for adulthood, for the prerogatives of being grown up. They want to look like men and women, to be treated like men and women, to be their own bosses. But this involves change, and change can be frightening. At the very least, change is stressful. Studies have shown that even changes supposedly for the better cause stress. Surprisingly enough, such happy experiences as getting married, getting a raise or a promotion, taking a vacation, having a baby, all cause a definite amount of stress. These experiences involve a change in the status quo, and any new experience, even those avidly sought, can cause heart flutters, uneasy stomachs, and general worriment.

Changes that adolescents experience are very different from those in adult life. Adults have past experiences to draw on. But when you move from childhood to adulthood there are no past experiences to draw on; it's all *new*. If changes make adults nervous, you can imagine what it must be like to change into a whole new person! You don't have to *imagine* it—if you're an adolescent, that's exactly what is happening to you.

A teenager's body often seems to be running away from him or her. Who is this new person? Do I like my looks, or do I hate the way I look? Am I tall enough? Are my breasts attractive? Has my nose suddenly grown too long? Is my cute little-girl's chin suddenly too short, sort of receding? In the fifth grade, everybody was cute as a button. Five years later hair is oily, pimples are rampant, fat isn't cute anymore, growing arms and legs respond awkwardly. But the individual teenager doesn't usually see that everybody is in the same boat. She can see only her own acne, her own fat or gawkiness. She or he feels unattractive, different, not in control of what is happening. The pimples keep popping, things keep getting knocked over, no matter what he does.

And if the outside of the body is trouble, how about the inside? What are these new sexual feelings—the girl's need for masculine vibrations, the boy's irresistible physical urges? It sometimes seems that all of one's emotions have become superheated. The lows are so terribly low, the highs are so high. The fears are so frightening. The anger is so overwhelming. The guilts are so consuming. No wonder many kids feel they're off the wall, flipping out.

His own body is only part of this strange new world in which the adolescent finds himself. Actually, it's the same world, but confusingly altered. The people are the same, but so different. One's parents are the same people, but their expectations are different. They expect much more. Teachers no longer look on misbehavior as a bit of high-spiritedness expected in a kid. Now they demand the conduct of an adult. The corner grocer no longer chucks one under the chin; now he expects the boys to act like men, and he may even flirt with the girls. Everyone is the same, but everyone is so different. And this too is a loss.

Your entire social life is changing. Though you always had friends of your own age, your family was most important. The way Dad and Mom felt mattered above everything else. They were the ones you looked to for guidance, support, love. But now, as you turn that corner of twelve or thirteen, you're taking another look at your parents. You're no longer so sure they have all the answers. And you're thinking that the answers they have may not necessarily be the ones for you right now. Sometimes they don't seem to understand, or even know, what's going on in your world.

Your peers—other adolescents—are rapidly becoming the most significant people in your life. You care what they think more than you ever did before. It's so important to be popular, to be liked by them, to be respected. Their opinions on everything are most important to you. And yet, they are as confused as you are, for the new world you are all growing into seems shifting, insecure. So if you've lost much of your confidence in your parents, and you can't really rely on your peers, where can you turn?

And you're coming into contact with the larger world more than you did before. You're thinking more about what is going on in that world. You can see how far removed reality is from the ideal. In the past, school, home, and the neighborhood were the boundaries of your world. No longer. Your ways of thinking are changing, your imagination is developing. You no longer see just what is there before your eyes. Your mind ranges over worlds you haven't seen, things you've only heard of vaguely. You imagine how these things should be, and you're confused, anxious, even angry that they are not that way, that you're alive in such an imperfect world. And this is a subject for countless rap sessions with the other kids, none of which result in comforting answers.

The adolescent of today has even more of a monkey on his back than in the past. Until recently, the world of adult values has been fairly unchanging, but now things are shifting so fast that even adults are confused. People are no longer so sure of their attitudes about sex, patriotism, religion, work, possessions as they once were. Many people wonder if marriage, or even monogamy, is the answer for everyone. Or is heterosexuality, for that matter, right for everyone? Is loyalty to one's nation, one's particular political slice of the world, more important than loyalty to humanity as a whole? The established religions often seem to be crumbling, with new approaches to spirituality being explored by more and more people. Is the work ethic the last word in our mundane world? What about people who can't get work, people who can't get the proper training and education to get good jobs? Are people being paid properly for the work they do? Is ownership of houses, cars, boats, jewelry, and all the paraphernalia of our modern world the key to happiness? Adults are questioning many of the answers they were so sure of before. And if grown-ups are not sure of the answers, adolescents have even more reason to wonder what's coming down.

During the past decade even the roles and expectations of men and women have been changing. More and more frequently, a woman's primary function is no longer that of caretaker of the home and children; a man's primary function is no longer that of breadwinner. Qualities previously considered masculine, such as assertiveness, or feminine, such as tenderness, now are considered appropriate for both men and women. Women are encouraged to pursue careers—not just caretaking or assisting positions while they wait for men to ask for their hands in marriage—but careers previously considered masculine. Women are becoming engineers, physicians, business executives. Conversely, men are now expected to share some of the caretaking responsibilities in marriage—of the children, of the home. Some men have even taken leaves from their work to care for newborn children so that their wives may return to work earlier.

With these many new options, choices have expanded drastically. Questions about standards and values are rampant. The adolescent, who is faced with choices and decisions, finds himself in a changing world, with shifting standards and values, at a time when he feels safer with the known and tested verities. This can only compound his feelings of being adrift, with no safe harbor in sight.

The media reflect the confusion of values that is so much a part of today's world. Newspapers, television, movies, magazines constantly consider these questions, using both factual and fictional approaches. We are saturated by these themes, with problems and questions coming at us from all directions. The media compound the confusion, and young people, in particular, now find no baseline of accepted wisdom against which they can test themselves.

The teens are without doubt among the most confusing

and stressful times of life, because the developmental tasks are so great. Many adolescents don't even recognize when they're depressed. One of the first steps toward licking a problem is to recognize that problem. Then you can start doing something about it.

2/Avoiding
the Big Problem

When most people think of depression they think of a hapless individual dragging around in slow motion with his chin down to his knees. He has trouble talking to people. He can't sleep. He has no appetite. He may be constipated. Often he is on the verge of tears or may cry for long periods. He may bemoan his fate or, even more likely, keep his misery bottled up inside. He wonders if life is worth living and may be obsessed with thoughts of suicide. He may feel his family and friends would be better off without him. He is the living personification of the comic strip character who went around with his own personal cloud perpetually raining on him.

Although some depressed people do act and feel like this, there are other ways to express depression. Many adolescents do not experience this all-is-lost, goodbye-cruel-world type of depression. They tend to hide their depression. Depressed? Absolutely not! That would be telling the world you aren't measuring up. Depressed, when you are right in the middle of the happiest years of your life? What a failure! What a shameful thing! Many teenagers can never let anyone know they're depressed.

A person with the chin-on-the-ground syndrome is experiencing what psychotherapists call a "clinical depression." He is exhibiting symptoms that most people associate with depression—he *knows* he is depressed. But adolescents don't usually look or feel this way. As we have seen, they are more likely to express their conflicts in other ways. It's only as they move into later adolescence that they more likely feel a clinical depression. Some of the ways in which adolescents express depression are called "depressive equivalents." Who would ever suspect that Amy, Most Popular Girl in School, or Bill, Big Man on Campus, are depressed?

During the day, in school, Amy feels good. Her boyfriend is attentive. She takes part in the Student Council meeting. She talks animatedly in the cafeteria and on the way home with the girls. She's the picture of the happy young lady—just what her parents want.

And that's Amy's problem. She's not living her own life: she's living her parents' version of her life. When she's home alone in her room, she often feels restless. She doesn't like to be alone. She picks up the phone and calls one of the kids. "I'm bored," she says. "What are you doing?" Amy needs constant stimulation, constant reassurance from other people that the role she is playing is convincing. And it *is* convincing—except to herself. Something is wrong, she senses. Something is missing. She often feels empty.

Amy doesn't quite *feel* her depression. She feels something else—she feels the depressive equivalents. She feels boredom, restlessness, has to be constantly busy. She may feel that she's different from the other kids. But if you asked her if she were depressed, she'd say, "Who me? Never!"

Bill is also playing a role—a role to get something from other people. Only Bill isn't trying to please his parents. Bill is hung up on being popular, on being the guy all the other kids admire. Bill is a popularity junkie.

When you stop to think about it, "junkie" is a good word for someone trying to find happiness from outside sources. The sources could be drugs, booze, too much work, sexual promiscuity, too much play, other people's approval, any number of things. The point is that the junkie's source of calmness and happiness is not within himself. It comes from the outside world. And the outside world never gives you exactly what you need. You're the only one who can do that.

As a result, Bill often feels restless and bored. He has to keep seeking new entertainment so that he doesn't feel this restlessness and boredom. He has to make another touchdown, another basket, another team. He has to win yet another prize. He has to get yet another girl. He may continue this same pattern all his life. He may die at fifty-five from a heart attack, miserable and dissatisfied with what the world considers his success. Somewhere along the line he sold himself a bill of goods, and it started when he was a kid.

Bill feels good while he's playing ball and being outstanding at it, or when he walks down the corridor and the girls' heads turn, or when the votes are counted and he's the class president again. But this is momentary and soon passes. When he's alone, he doesn't feel very good at all. He's left with himself, and that's awful. If only he could get away from himself—but of course he can't. None of us can.

There are many other ways of being down, bummed out, fed up. And they all feel rotten. Some teenagers frantically seek new hobbies, new games, new things to do. Almost as soon as they take something up, they drop it. They lose interest. This is marvelous for manufacturers of games, sporting equipment, clothing, and whatnot, but it's not much of a way to run one's life. It's nothing but a series of dead ends. Parents complain bitterly about the money such shenanigans cost them, but it's a rare parent who realizes that his son or daughter is desperately trying to run from depression and that his or her on-again-off-again behavior is an expression of a depressive equivalent.

Miriam, the Grind, feels exhausted most of the time. If you observe her when she doesn't know she's being looked at, you'll see that every line of her face and body seems to be sagging. She has trouble getting to sleep at night. She has trouble staying asleep. When morning comes, she faces the day utterly dragged out. If you ask her how she feels, she'll probably say, "I'm really beat today." Actually, she's beat every day. Miriam is experiencing a frequent symptom of depression—exhaustion.

You can feel exhausted even if you are getting eight hours' sleep each night. When you wake up you're still tired. Even a nap after school doesn't seem to help. So much energy is going into preoccupation with your problems that you're really tired out. Moreover, for a depressed person sleep can be especially inviting. It can be a way of withdrawing from waking life, from the nagging problems. Depressed people often spend an inordinate amount of time withdrawing into sleep.

Preoccupation with inner maladjustments can have other effects than physical tiredness. Miriam has to go over and over her studies to make them sink in. She's so worried about herself that it's no wonder she has only a part of her mind to devote to the matter at hand—what is on the printed page in front of her. She realizes that she has to study longer and harder than most people to get good marks. Maybe good marks will make her feel better about herself. But any joy they might give her is transitory. You can't win 'em all, every day—and Miriam's negative feelings about herself can't be offset by honors and prizes.

Another danger is that Miriam may reach the point where she feels that this compulsive, inefficient pounding of the books is just too much. She may feel it's not worth it, that she really isn't much of a student and could never make it through college. She may drop out of school. Many intelligent, motivated young people have become dropouts simply because they finally gave up trying to transcend the depressive equivalents that so hindered their efforts.

Did you ever know anyone who just couldn't wait? Who fidgeted in line more than most people? Who drove a car with his horn, who fumed at red lights and stop signs?

Who constantly bit his nails, tapped his foot? Nail biters, scratchers, fidgeters often are exhibiting agitation. They radiate tension and impatience. These traits can be signals of other maladjustments, but they are often symptoms of what is called an "agitated depression."

Hypochondriasis, or worry about physical symptoms, can also be evidence of depression. People like this find it safer to fret about imagined physical quirks than to face the real problem—how they feel about themselves. This is not a conscious decision; it's a way to avoid dealing with the *big* problem—what is wrong with them—for on some level they feel that there is no solution to this emotional problem, that it's simply too anxiety-provoking to face.

Some girls worry constantly about their menstrual periods. You probably know someone who is usually worried about a cold—the beginning of pneumonia?—or fretting about a sore throat—cancer? If his eyes are tired, he's going blind. If she has a headache, it might be a brain tumor.

The trouble is, your emotions *can* make you physically ill. A girl we'll call Joanne doesn't feel at ease, confident within herself. She must always have someone to reassure her that she is somebody, that she is worth something, that she is lovable. When Joanne loses a boyfriend, the bottom drops out of her emotional world. But rather than face depression, she unconsciously displaces her feelings onto somatic symptoms. In her case, it's an aching back—and it's a legitimate aching back. She becomes so tense that she really does have muscle spasms. She worries about the pain, and that contracts her muscles even more. But somewhere in the depths of her being, carefully hidden away from her conscious awareness, is the conviction that it's better to hurt physically than to face the fact that she doesn't much like herself and that losing a boyfriend is proof that she is unlovable.

Medical science now readily recognizes the interplay between the emotions and the body. Many illnesses are *psychosomatic*: they spring from emotional conflicts. Ulcers are an example. It's not what you're eating, the saying goes, it's what's eating you that causes those stomach upsets. Recent studies have shown that certain personality types—high-powered executives inordinately driven toward success, overwhelmingly ambitious, compulsively fretful about error—are prone to heart attacks. Depressed people whose energy sources are lowered are prone to colds and viruses.

A lack of appetite is a frequent symptom of depression. On the other hand, overeating can also be a symptom. The author Kurt Vonnegut once commented that it's hard to feel bad while you're eating. But when you overeat, you often feel guilty, which erodes your self-esteem further, which influences you to eat even more. It's just another one of those vicious circles. What all of us overeaters are doing is going back to Mommy's breast, that not-quite-forgotten time when mealtimes meant all was well and somebody loved you. It's a mixed bag: you're being good to yourself, but at the same time there's a built-in punishment—guilt. And aside from the health problems, in our culture fat just isn't chic.

The kids we've been looking at have turned their depressive problems in on themselves in one way or another, using their feelings or their bodies to express depression. Fred, the "bad kid" mentioned before, has turned his out toward his environment. Therapists call this "acting-out behavior." Fred has focused on the anger underlying a depression. He turns this anger outward. It is safer for him to blame the world and strike out against it than to grapple with his feelings about himself. Fred subconsciously feels that any activity, no matter how dangerous or destructive, is better than facing himself. The trouble with this kind of behavior is that it reinforces Fred's guilt and makes him feel even worse. Again, the vicious circle. Ripping off grocery stores, smoking pot in the boys' lavatory, painting dirty words on the town water tower doesn't help a depression much. In fact, it makes Fred feel worse.

Some adolescents who engage in antisocial behavior feel so guilty that they unconsciously arrange to be caught and punished. This assuages their guilt, leaving them free to express the anger again. And so the pattern starts over. This need for punishment, which is based in guilt and the resultant feelings of being "bad," is the result of trying to run from a depression.

But this pattern is not peculiar to persons who are acting out or who are antisocial or criminal. Are you someone who always gets caught if you break a parental or school rule? Laura had been told she was not to frequent a shopping mall where the local punks hung out. When her mother made her own weekly shopping trip to the mall, there was Laura. Laura knew that her mother went to the mall every Thursday. Now this seems stupid—but Laura is a very bright girl. Unconsciously, she had picked the night she would be caught. She had rebelled in anger but had also set herself up for punishment to assuage her guilt. This pattern reinforces her bad feelings about herself, and depression results.

Another form of acting out is sexual promiscuity. For some teenagers, sex spells acceptance. Somebody cares about them. And people like this are often unable to feel that someone cares for them except on the physical level, through sexual activity. Like Fred's antisocial behavior, however, sexual promiscuity doesn't work. It aggravates guilt, which further erodes self-esteem, leaving emptiness and depression.

In all of these ways in which kids express their depressive feelings, or defend themselves against them, there are certain common denominators. These are the feelings of helplessness, hopelessness, pessimism, poor self-esteem, anger, guilt. There are also feelings of isolation, alienation, being different, unique in a negative kind of way. The feeling that something is wrong with them shades all their perceptions of themselves and their world.

Acting out anger, overeating, worrying about health, and all the other ways people use to try to run away from depression just don't work. They are expressions of depressions, not cures. What can help? Knowledge of what could be causing the depression might—so let's see what causes a depression.

3/Loss:
The Start of Depression

There's a difference, of course, between the sort of depression that really flattens a person, that hangs on and becomes a serious, debilitating part of his life, and the plain old blues, the downs that everyone has from time to time.

Adolescence is prime time for emotional ups and downs. Many psychotherapists plan on seeing an adolescent several times before making a diagnosis of his emotional state, simply because an adolescent's emotions are so labile, so unstable. Young people are extreme in their mood swings. The highs are so high, the lows are so low, and they keep changing. So the blues for teenagers seem more intense than for people of other ages.

This emotional instability is part of being a teenager. It's part of having a changing body, a changing mind, changing relationships with the world. Change is stressful to anyone, and in the second decade of life change is constant.

19

Most of the time, when a person wakes up with the blues, he or she knows what is causing them. He got a D in chemistry. Her boyfriend took another girl to the movies. Dad is angry about that dent in the rear fender. These are things bound to befall anyone; they are par for the course in living. When one is down because of things like this, one knows this too shall pass. There will be other tests, other boyfriends, other fenders. And when you know something is temporary, it's not so hard to take—especially when you're pretty sure you know what's causing that blah feeling.

But even if you can't put your finger on what's causing these transitory blues, you still have perspective. You don't lose track of the positive aspects of your life. Whatever is wrong is only a small part of life. You can compensate. You may not be great in chemistry, but you're a good basketball player. Your boyfriend may have let you down, but you're heading for a college scholarship. The problem that's getting you down is not your whole life; it's not overwhelming. You're realistic; when you're blue, your perception of the world and people doesn't change or become distorted.

The blues are transitory. They come and they go. But a depression doesn't evaporate by the time you get to school, or even by lunchtime. Some people describe depression as a cloud descending, something happening to them they can do nothing about. They are overwhelmed by a feeling of helplessness. Everything is slowed up— thinking, moving. They may or may not know what is causing the weighty feeling, but it seems to pervade their whole world. Often it becomes progressively worse until the whole world seems black; nothing is right. When you are in the grip of a real depression, the positives just don't count. A string of A's, all the varsity letters the school has to give, the lead in the senior play just won't help. When you're depressed your perception of yourself and the world and people—their motives and feelings—is distorted. Everything is screened through feelings of hopelessness, helplessness, and eroded self-esteem. A real depression is not transitory. It lingers and lingers and lingers. When you're depressed, you could very well be in for a long haul—and this is also true when you're running away from a depression or expressing it through symptoms.

Depression in adolescents can be serious. The suicide rate in this age group has increased tenfold in recent decades. Suicide is the most serious, most evident manifestation of depression, but there is other behavior that is not so dramatically apparent, such as accident proneness and risk-taking. There are girls who constantly burn or cut themselves in the kitchen, boys who climb into the family car and play chicken. These external evidences of depression can encompass loss of appetite, overeating, sleep problems, personal sloppiness, neglect of school work or inability to function efficiently in school, withdrawal from social life, sexual promiscuity. Some adolescents have obsessions about death, feelings of guilt, hopelessness, helplessness, failure, humiliation, or worthlessness. Some even seem to hear a dead relative telling them they are bad or have vivid dreams of a relative berating them as that relative did when he was alive.

Sometimes their depressions may be masked as extreme hostility or aggressiveness.

Adolescence is a time of trying out new roles. It's part of the trip, part of finding out who this new person, this almost-adult who is suddenly inhabiting your skin, really is. And so it's natural for the teenager to intensify any new feeling that comes along, and this includes depression. I'm sad? I'll really feel it. She goes into her room, locks the door, and puts on sad records. Maybe she's really not very sad to start with, but if the song is sad, she'll become sad. At this time of life one's sense of self, what is called the "ego boundaries," are fluid. A teenager can identify very readily with people or situations outside of herself. She can live the words of a song. She can become the person in the song. She may enjoy the exquisite hurt.

Another reason for intensifying feelings—sad or happy —or playing different roles is the underlying feeling of emptiness many adolescents experience. This emptiness— another expression of depression—is the result of the changes the adolescent is experiencing and with which he feels he does not have the resources to cope. He has no confidence in himself, feels isolated and bereft—empty. And so to fill the emptiness, to help define who he is, he intensifies his feelings. In some ways, this is running away from the real questions about who he is, what he is.

Some adolescents try to fill up the emptiness and still the dread and anxiety by getting drunk or popping pills. But the emptiness, the anxiety, the dread continue, requiring more booze, more drugs. Although teenagers involved in this will tell you it's fun, it's not—it's a suicidal equivalent!

Real depression is anything but fun, anything but a game. It not only involves the depressed person, it affects the people around him. They feel as helpless and as hopeless as he does. And because of these feelings, they become frustrated and impatient with him. They tend to give advice that doesn't help. A classic example is Lucy's psychiatric advice in "Peanuts"—"Snap out of it! Five cents, please."

People tend to avoid people who are depressed. This increases loneliness, alienation, feelings of worthlessness, depression. Another of those vicious circles. Even when people go out of their way to be nice to poor sad Sam he doesn't feel he deserves this treatment. It intensifies his guilt, his bad feelings about himself, and his hopelessness.

Shaking a depression is no easy matter. How can you overcome the feelings of helplessness and hopelessness, or recognize when you are defending against a depression? A good start is to understand just what a depression is and what causes it.

A *depression* is a mourning process gone askew. That's the way the psychotherapists put it. And what is mourning? *Mourning* is an emotional process in which we work through, and ultimately accept, a loss. This loss, in the popular mind, is usually associated with death, with the loss of a loved one. But it need not be: it can also relate to loss of something else in one's life. The person who is mourning in a healthy manner recognizes there has been a loss. While he is working through this loss, he still perceives the world and himself realistically and is able to follow through on his daily routines. The depressed

person, however, is completely preoccupied with the
loss, with the feeling of sadness and grief.

In the context of adolescence, the loss can be the loss of
childhood or, as the poets put it, the loss of innocence. It
can be the loss of self-esteem, of confidence in one's self; it
can be the feeling that one can't live up to one's own
expectations of oneself.

There are certain healthy ways of handling a loss, a
series of steps and processes. Collectively, these are
known as the "mourning process."

First, after the loss, there is denial. Everyone experiences this. When hurtful things happen, we tend to deny
them. The greater the hurt, the more we deny it. We tend
to forget hurtful things and remember pleasurable things.
When we are hurt, we run away from the memory to a
greater or lesser degree. If someone dies, you tell yourself
it didn't happen, that he's just gone on a trip. If your
parents divorce, you tell yourself they will get back together again. Denial is a person's way of defending himself. It is called a "mechanism of defense"—a defense
against a hurt that a person cannot readily absorb. It's a
protection.

After the initial denial of the loss, there begins to seep
through an awareness of reality. Your parents really are
divorced, they really aren't living together; your father
isn't coming home from a business trip. And with that
awareness, you feel angry at this traumatic change, this
loss. The underlying cause of this anger is the helplessness
and hurt that you feel. You have absolutely no control
over a loved one's life or death; your parents did not con-

sult you when they broke up. So you turn your anger against the person who you feel has caused this loss—your mother for dying, your parents for splitting, perhaps your parents for moving away from a neighborhood where you knew everyone and felt comfortable. During this angry stage the focus is on what has been taken from you, what you no longer have. You are preoccupied with the loss and what it means to you.

At this point, you will probably try a little "bargaining" with God or the fates. Dear God, you may think, if you'll let me off this hook, if you'll let my parents get back together, I'll never fight with them again. If you'll fix it so we move back to the old town, I'll never cut classes again. But the bargaining doesn't work and the anger is intensified. It's another vicious circle. This is the anger that is the basis for a lot of acting-out behavior. The world is being paid back for the hurts and losses.

But very often one feels, along with this anger, that one has no right to feel this way. How can you be angry with someone who has died? He didn't choose that fate. How can you be angry with parents who have worked to make you comfortable and who feel a move is part of that? Anger is a feeling we've all been taught is "not nice." So along with the anger, you feel guilty. And the guilt may spread. You may feel you are bad because of your feelings, and this is an erosion of self-esteem.

Betsy is a woman of thirty who is seeing a psychotherapist because she can never express anger, and this bottling-up of her feelings is having adverse effects on her health, emotionally and physically. Her problem goes back to her teenage years, when, as all teenagers do in a healthy course of development, she was trying to break away from her dependence on her parents. One of the ways adolescents break away from their parents is by being angry with them, by devaluating them. Betsy was able to feel anger toward her father—he sometimes told her she was stupid. But her mother was another story. Her mother was a kind of plaster saint. She never showed anger, never spoke slightingly of anyone. To be angry at such a person would, Betsy felt, be a terrible thing. But at her time of life, adolescence, it would have been "normal" for her to be angry at her mother. She bottled up her anger, denied it, and ten years later she realized she had shut off *all* her feelings. She was an emotional zombie, and this brought her to the psychotherapist's office. Basically, she was chronically depressed.

The aspects of mourning—denial, anger, guilt—are not emotions that one necessarily experiences in a separate manner, one after another. A person can deny, and at the next moment feel angry, and also have a constant, pervasive sense of guilt. You can almost simultaneously forget that your father isn't going to go to the baseball game with you, feel angry with him, and feel guilty about being angry. Our emotions work in subtle, fluid, complex ways. They certainly don't line up in an orderly, neat, conscious way. All these feelings are "normal." But if the feelings are *too* intense, and if a person gets caught in them, a depression can develop.

In a healthy working-through of mourning, even though you recognize these feelings as strange and are not terribly proud of them, you know they are only a small part of you. You live with them. You know you are not going to act on them. They don't erode your confidence in yourself, your feelings of self-esteem. Gradually these negative feelings dissipate. You grieve, but you get on with your life. You have come to terms with loss, have accepted it. It becomes a part of your past. You are not fighting reality anymore; you are living in the present. You are not preoccupied with the loss. There is a feeling of sadness, but this is quite different from depression.

A depression—as opposed to a healthy working-through of a loss—happens when you are stuck in the mourning process. The younger adolescent—below the age of fifteen or so—may well react in a different way than the older adolescent. The younger person is more likely to deny what has happened, to run away from his problem, and act out his anger. This is the time for explosions within the family and destructive acts against society. Negative behavior reinforces the guilt of the young adolescent, makes him feel even more a bad person, and may thrust him into further destructive, antisocial activity that helps him run away from his feelings about himself. He is caught in the denial and anger.

The anger seeps out against his environment, against other people. Even more important, it turns back on himself. He begins to feel that he is a terrible person. He is punishing the world, but he is punishing himself at the same time.

This response is not limited to younger adolescents but may be seen in an eighteen-year-old whose emotional development does not match his chronological age. However, the older adolescent usually has a different response to loss. She may feel apathetic, worthless, be caught up in the physical and mental slowdown that is characteristic of depression. She may feel bored, restless, tired, which are depressive equivalents. In other words, her way of coping tends to be internal, rather than directed outward, as is usually the case with younger adolescents.

The important difference between a mourning process and depression is the effect on the individual, his perception of himself and others. A successful mourning can be an enriching experience in which an individual accepts his frailties, mortality, and vulnerabilities. The final acceptance is of himself in the scheme of living and dying. One who is depressed has not accepted the loss, has not worked it through and moved on in his living. A depressed person is caught up with the loss. His energies are invested in denying, or being enraged, and feeling guilty. As a result, his feelings of self-esteem and confidence are eroded. He feels helpless and hopeless. The greater the guilt, the worse he feels about himself. He may not feel the anger; he may only feel that he is "bad," unlikeable, unlovable, not deserving, worthless. In this way he turns his anger back on himself.

Losses occur at all ages. We have constant losses throughout our lives, of one sort or another. It is one of the givens of being alive. What most people don't realize is that each loss, and the way we work it through, affects how we work through every subsequent loss. A loss before a child is able to speak and understand—the death of a mother, an accident in which the child is severely injured, perhaps crippled—is all the more devastating because it cannot be understood by the child. It will affect the way the individual handles losses throughout his entire life. It will color his whole character and his view of the world. People who have had these early, preverbal losses often have what therapists call a depressive core. These are people who tend to be extremely pessimistic, who expect the worst to happen, and who are constantly on guard against it. They are not really comfortable when things are going well. Often they cannot form relationships.

Studies have shown that some institutionalized infants who, after a period of successful mothering, are then denied the love and mothering a baby needs have literally given up on life. They died because they were depressed. They withdrew from responding to others, even from taking nourishment. Infants who have been neglected from birth, if they live, tend to become delinquents.

Children below the age of adolescence do not show the usual symptoms of depression. They may cry and become sad, but they do not mourn. A seven year old may go outdoors to play during her mother's funeral. Since adolescence is a time of reworking things that have happened to us previously, sometimes depression that seems to come out of the blue is really a reaction to conflicts, traumas, and losses experienced years before.

The most important loss for an adolescent is the changing relationship with his parents. You're no longer a cutie of eight or nine. Now you're growing into an adult, and your parents' attitudes are shifting, sometimes in a very confusing way. Sometimes it's hard to figure out what on earth they *do* want of you. At one moment you're told you're too old to act a certain way—at another that you're too young to stay out after ten. Very possibly they're not sure themselves.

And if you feel that you are disappointing your parents, that you've lost their approval—whether you actually have or not—that is a real loss. When you were a little kid, you felt you had their unconditional love, that they loved you just because you were you. Now they frown at the length of your hair, your torn jeans, your room, and often your friends. As a developing adult, you are expected to meet certain standards in appearance, behavior, and responsibilities—and parents are usually quite vocal in expressing their expectations and disappointments. The change from unconditional love to "love with strings" is a loss with which many adolescents have difficulty coping.

This loss of confidence works two ways. The teenager not only feels he may not be getting the love and acceptance his parents formerly showered on him, he may well be taking some new looks at the parents themselves. They are no longer Mr. and Mrs. Right, Mr. and Mrs. Wonderful. He now sees flaws here and there—in fact, some days in every little thing they say and do. He may even be ashamed of his parents in some ways. He is literally part and parcel of his parents; they created him, not only in body, but substantially in personality. And if they're not so great, he thinks wryly, what does that make him?

Jean, age fourteen, had always been proud of her family name and of being the daughter of a well-known business-man. Then she began to believe that other business people in the community did not hold her father in great respect and that possibly he had some questionable practices. He had a habit of saying that he had sometimes been two steps ahead of the sheriff. By this he meant that he was a businessman of courage, who wasn't afraid to take a chance and go out on a limb in developing new projects. But Jean misinterpreted this harmless boast of her fa-ther's. She began to think that it meant he had not always been honest. A pervasive sense of shame enveloped her. The shame contaminated her sense of herself, eroded her self-esteem, and left her depressed. This two-way loosen-ing of the loving family bond represents not only a loss of love but may also engender loss of confidence in the adolescent.

The teenager may also feel he is losing the respect of the other kids—his peer group—and that too is a jolting experience—whether you actually have lost their respect or just think you have.

But the most important person whose love and respect you need is not your parents or your peers, or anyone else on your horizon—it's yourself. And many adolescents set their goals so high, make their idealized image so perfect, that it is impossible to live up to their own expectations of themselves. A healthy adolescent will have expectations of himself that are realistic, that are not impossible for him to attain. But if the way a teenager actually is and his ideal image of himself are so far apart that there is no chance for them to come together, then that person is in trouble. He has lost pride in himself; he has lost the most important love of all.

It's hard for a teenager to know who he is, what to expect of himself. For twelve years he had a definite role —he was a kid. He was a son, she was a daughter. He and she were born for the part. But now—who am I? A nurse, an astronaut, a professor, a hippie, the ingenue or leading man, or the comedienne or hero's best friend? And, having lost this secure sense of self, of being a kid, the adolescent is searching, even flailing about, for his new role, his adulthood.

Not only is he changing, his entire perception of the world is, too. His mind is now working differently. His imagination is developing, his intellect is maturing. He is able to contemplate the future and tries to place himself there. The old, secure baselines are now wavering. The blacks are not so black, the whites not so white. There are grays in between. For example, when he gets up in the morning and his mother sets a bowl of cereal in front of him, it's no longer just a bowl of cereal. How many people in the world, he wonders, don't have a bowl of cereal? How many are going hungry, even starving? Is this cereal good for him? What is its nutritional content? What about the additives? Are there things in it that are bad for his body? Life is no longer so simple, and this realization brings with it a loss of security.

When these losses occur, some teenagers tend to deny what is happening. Amy puts on a happy face—what the psychotherapists call a "smiling depression." She has lost the unconditional love of her parents that she had when she was small. Now she feels—very possibly falsely—that she has to buy their love.

Bill is doing the same thing, in a more indirect way. He struts around, Big Man on Campus. He has substituted the peer group for his parents. But he too feels he must buy affection. Amy and Bill have not yet discovered who they really are, their sense of self. Unconsciously, they have denied the real issue—that is, how to be separate and unique individuals, and accept responsibility for their uniqueness.

Anger and guilt are prominent factors in the behavior of Fred, the determined juvenile delinquent. Somewhere along the line, Fred has felt a loss. Perhaps it is his moving into adolescence, moving away from childhood and the more or less automatic love a child is given. Perhaps even from his early years his parents have never given him the love and acceptance a child needs. Rather than face this loss, Fred feels anger and lets it spill out against everyone. He gets into fights, he breaks things up, rips things off. Of course, he doesn't get much approval for this—except perhaps a few pats on the back from other vandals, who are as mixed up and miserable as he is. Rather than face his feelings about himself, Fred finds it safest to feel and express anger. Tonight he'll rip off another grocery store. But underneath is a troubling sense of his own badness that reinforces his anger and impels his flight to antisocial behavior.

Many kids who go the juvenile delinquent route are constantly getting caught. On some unconscious level, they are setting things up so they'll be caught and punished. When we feel we're bad, we tend to find ways to punish ourselves.

Often this method of handling guilt—punishing oneself —is perpetuated throughout a person's life. That's what's behind the self-destructive behavior of compulsive smokers, junkies, alcoholics, gamblers. These people are setting themselves up to lose. At the most extreme, criminal level, penitentiaries are filled with people like this. This behavior has nothing to do with people's intelligence; it has everything to do with their emotional patterns. They express anger at the world and then punish themselves for being bad.

The ultimate angry gesture, the final self-destructive act, is suicide. For a person with this guilt-ridden emotional set, suicide can be irresistible, for it not only punishes oneself but also punishes the people around one.

Few adolescents go to the extremes we've been discussing, but many are aware of their anger and feel guilty because of it. And the guilt erodes self-confidence and self-respect. It is the anger and guilt, then, that cause the problem.

Kids sometimes feel so different—and in an unhealthy way. It's fine to feel that your individuality is different from everyone else's, that you are unique. Feeling that way, and being glad about it, is a plus. A lot of kids, because of their guilt, which colors their perceptions of themselves, feel instead that they are strange, inferior, that they don't measure up in some way, that they're weird. They don't meet their own expectations and also feel they don't meet others' expectations of what a teen-ager should be.

You don't have to feel that way. There are healthy ways to handle the adolescent's occupational disease—depres-sion. Of course, there is no way to avoid losses as you move from childhood into adulthood, into this confusing new world. But if you can understand better what is hap-pening to you, the problems you are facing, your chang-ing roles with your parents, with other people, and above all with yourself, you have a better chance of coming through adolescence in one healthy piece. So let's take a look at some of the pressures that line up to bug a kid in his teens.

4/Outgrowing the Nest

The adolescent's main problem with his family is that his parents knew him when he was a child. Now he is thrust into new roles, and his parents must adjust to this new person. They must try to forget the baby, the small child, the older child. What they have on their hands now is part adult, part child. In fact, what is it? There never was a parent who didn't distractedly ask this question of himself, his spouse, and anyone else who would listen. In fact, you are asking this very question of yourself: Who on earth am I?

The hard part is that this transformation doesn't happen all at once. A person isn't a child one day, an adult the next. If this were the case, it might be startling, traumatic, magical, and a few other strange things, but it might well be easier. The shock would be over in a day, or a few. But you know that it doesn't work that way. It's tantalizingly gradual, confusingly back and forth, this mysterious growth from childhood into adulthood. You really can't blame your parents for being upset and puzzled. But of course you wouldn't be human—especially a human teenager—if you didn't.

What the adolescent and his family are going through at this point is traumatic under the best conditions. It is a break from the past, a change. Any change, particularly such a revolutionary, uncharted one as this, is stressful, even when things are at their best. When family life, like most other things, is slightly or markedly askew, your relationships with your father and mother can get a bit, sometimes *quite* a bit, out of control.

As an adolescent, what is your goal regarding your family? Baldly stated, your ultimate goal is to get out of it. Eventually, you want to spread your wings and fly away from the nest. For the time being, you want to be treated as an adult within the family. But it's not all that easy, from either the adolescent's or the parents' side of the nest.

Yet, you must make this change, unless you're going to go through life in the shadow of your mother and/or father—a mama's boy at forty, daddy's girl till you're chronologically and biologically a grandmother. You must stake out your own territory, establish an identity of your own, separate from your parents. Now is the time of struggle to develop into your own adult personality. Under the best of conditions, it's no easy task.

First, you must choose and prepare for an occupation. Do you want college? Do you want a job? Do you want technical school?

Second, you must prepare for your sexual role. What is it to be a man? What is it to be a woman? What are the responsibilities? What are the privileges?

Third, you will choose how you are going to relate to other people as an adult. Will you be a leader or a follower, a victim or perhaps a victimizer? Will you be emotionally close to people or aloof?

Fourth, you must adopt a life-style. Will you be married; will you be single? Will you establish a home and family; will you join a commune? The world today gives the teenager more choices than ever before, and although this is good in many ways, it also forces individual decisions, with accompanying stress.

Much of your time as an adolescent is spent looking inward, asking yourself; who am I? Some of your time is spent looking outward: Where do I fit? And you are looking for significant others outside the family—whom can I love, who can love me? The resolution of these questions requires a reintegration and reorganization of the total personality as you move from being a child with few decisions to an adult responsible for yourself and capable of making your own decisions.

In order to begin to make choices, you must rework your relationships with your family. Now you're dependent, but you want to be independent. Of course, no one ever completely achieves independence, and perhaps one wouldn't want to, but to be a healthy adult, one must take long steps along this road, must resolve as much as he can his dependent-independent struggle. One can be *autonomous*—have a secure sense of oneself, be responsible for one's own decisions—and still need others in a healthy way.

Although we change—and quickly and radically during

the adolescent period—we always carry within us our history. A man of seventy has in him parts of the child he once was. We cannot ignore what has gone before—our childhood and its influence on our values, our choices, our personalities.

The human child has the longest period of dependency of any species on earth. A baby is completely helpless. As the child grows, he becomes more independent, but until adulthood he would be lost without the help of adults— specifically his parents. And he needs not just physical, material help. Perhaps even more significantly, he needs emotional support—guidance, protection, love.

Within this dependent situation, within the family triangle, the child has some internal tasks to perform. The boy must begin to learn to be a man—what society considers a man should be. The girl must begin to learn the womanly role she will play in society as an adult.

What you are as an adult is the sum total of everything that has happened to you in your past, but there are two times, childhood and adolescence, that are particularly significant in the development of your identity, the shaping of your selfhood.

The first period, from about the ages of four to six, is a precursor of the later, adolescent period. Both these periods involve the person's changing relationships with his parents. Up until about the age of two and a half, the primary relationship, for boy or girl, is with the mother. About that time, the child begins to move gradually out of the family, via playmates, nursery school, and so on, and becomes somewhat autonomous. Within the family unit, the child is beginning to come to terms with the reality of his position. Previously, he had perceived himself as being the center of his mother's world. Now he sees that his mother has a relationship with his father. His father kisses her when he comes home from work; they sleep together; they do things together without him. The little boy and the little girl both have the same task at this point—to adjust their relationships as they come to see the reality of the family situation. However, their methods of doing so are slightly different, and this is the beginning of sexual identification.

In this family romance, the boy must renounce his desire for the mother's total attention and love. He does this partly out of fear and partly out of guilt. He fears this huge male who is his rival for Mother's attention. This person, if provoked, could do him great harm—he has no chance to win in a battle. But the anger within him, these negative feelings toward his father, also make him feel guilty.

This internal struggle causes changes in the child's behavior, thought, and personality. During this process, he develops a conscience, and also an ideal image of himself. He begins to identify with the traits of his father that he perceives that his mother likes. Being like the father, the little boy feels, is what it is to be a man. Being like his father will procure for him the approval of his mother. This is the beginning of identification with the father. He begins to accept the prohibitions and restrictions that are inherent in family life. This is the beginning of the exercise of conscience.

The girl's task at this age is a little more complicated. She is dependent on the mother, and will continue to be so, but she is becoming increasingly needful of the father's approval and love. She finds herself becoming the rival of her mother. This rivalry, side by side with the continuing dependency on the mother, can cause increased stress for the girl. It is this conflict between dependency and rivalry that is the basis for so much antagonism, in adolescence, between mothers and daughters.

The small girl resolves this conflict in the same way as the boy: she begins to identify with the parent of the same sex—her mother—to win her father's approval and love. In the process she too develops a conscience and an ideal image of herself.

The conscience might be said to encompass the negative aspects in this striving situation—the prohibitions and restrictions. You don't kill your father if you're a boy; you don't kill your mother if you're a girl; you don't do away with your brothers and sisters. There are, the small child is learning, right ways and wrong ways of dealing with other people. The conscience makes us feel guilty.

The ideal image, on the other hand, refers to the positives—what you'd like to be like. At this stage, the ideal image is related directly to how the child perceives the parent of the same sex.

This period, for both boy and girl, is generally called the Oedipal period, a term originated by Sigmund Freud. It refers to the Greek mythological hero, Oedipus, who killed his father and married his mother. Differentiating between the sexes, Freud called the equivalent girl's experience the Electra period, named for the figure in Greek mythology who urged her brother to slay their mother, after the mother had killed their father.

This early working-through of changing relationships is a cornerstone in the individual's emotional development. Failure to resolve these conflicts satisfactorily intensifies the problem of coming to terms with your self—your identity during adolescence.

One of the major tasks in surviving adolescence is the reworking of the Oedipal. You are growing up, physically and intellectually. You are becoming a different person, and the world's attitudes toward you, as well as your own perceptions of the world, are changing. The core of your world, up to now, has been the family, particularly your mother and father, so any adjustments and alterations you make must be primarily in your attitudes toward your parents.

First, how do you separate from these two adults who have been, up to now, overwhelmingly the most important people in your life—models and sources of approval, disapproval, and love? How do you become your own person? How do you attain your own sense of uniqueness, and not become a carbon copy of your parents? How do you achieve a sense of selfhood with which you can be comfortable?

This attempt to separate is often the basis for anger and guilt so characteristic of adolescence, which can be underlying causes of depression.

The period of life from about the ages of seven to eleven has been referred to as the "latency period." During this time the child's emotional conflicts are relatively dormant. His energies are freed for the tasks of mastering his world, both intellectually and physically. It is a time for him to build confidence in himself. Can he or she ride a bicycle, climb a tree, wrestle, play ball? It is a time of learning to read, do math, negotiate the bus or subway system. The child is gradually, tentatively, moving out into the world. But his primary place of reference is the family, and he has to settle the relationships within the family before he can become his own person.

In early adolescence, at the time of puberty, there is a dramatic upsurge in sexual feeling. Because the child is still family-oriented, these feelings revolve around the parents. The girl thinks her father is the strongest, wisest, most attractive man in the world. The boy thinks his mother is the best-looking, best-cooking woman on the block. But very quickly the closeness to the family becomes frightening. Incest—sexual love for a family member—is one of our taboos. The child learned this some half a dozen years before, during the Oedipal period, when these feelings were repressed.

So, with some degree of panic, or at the very least with feelings of discomfort, he or she moves away from the parent of the opposite sex. He or she will feel uncomfortable with that parent. There is, in fact, a distancing from both the parents, a search for substitutes in the outside world. He or she doesn't recognize that these feelings of discomfort are based on sexual feelings involving the significant parent. The family is devalued. The boy or girl seeks other models, other sources of satisfaction. This is the time when the adolescent feels his greatest anger toward his parents. He feels so different from them he may even wonder if he's adopted.

To devalue the parents too abruptly, however, to throw out their value standards too precipitously, or to negate their authority too quickly leads to guilt, lowered self-esteem, and depression.

Fred, the juvenile delinquent, is experiencing this conflict. Fred's mother does not respect his father. Fred, therefore, is left high and dry, without a model to pattern himself after. In fact, since his father is a relatively solid citizen, Fred has turned in the opposite direction. Since his father respects private property, Fred covers it with graffiti. Since the father takes a dim view of theft, Fred rips off grocery stores or gas stations. The motivating force behind Fred's antisocial activities is anger because he has been deprived of a model and therefore devalued as a man.

Yet, Fred knows this isn't the right thing to do, by the standards of society, of his father, of most of his peers. And so he is mired in guilt, and his self-esteem plummets. This leads to depression or running away from himself and depression through more antisocial activity.

On the other hand, Amy, Most Popular Girl in School, has gone a different way. She fears to take any initiative, to defy or even move away slightly from her parents. What Daddy in particular wants goes, with Amy asking no question, at least consciously. She is the pretty, popular, socially active girl whom her parents delight in. But she doesn't delight in herself. She smiles, smiles, smiles, and does a marvelous impression of a Barbie Doll, but she certainly isn't smiling inside. She is angry; she is not her own person. She feels like a phony. She doesn't know who she is. She is depressed.

The better-adjusted young adolescent is not doing Fred's thing—throwing the baby out with the bathwater —or Amy's thing—clinging desperately to her dependency on Daddy and Mommy. The young teenager who is making it with a minimum of difficulty is gradually moving away from the family. His peers become important to him. Their approval means very much. Adult models outside the family—a teacher, a coach, a famous athlete, an admired public figure, a friend's parents—become increasingly important.

These people outside the family are giving you an idea of what you want to be like. Their influence dilutes the hold that the family once had on you. You can now move away from your parents, but not into a vacuum. You are moving meaningfully into the wider world of which you will, in normal development, become a part. The standards and values of these new important people in your life sometimes call into question those of your parents, which up to now you have accepted as holy writ. This is the beginning of your attempt at independence from your family, the beginning of a separate identity. Your ideals, your conscience, your sense of self will be unique. It will reflect your parents' influence but also the influence of many other significant people and forces.

How often, at this stage, have you upset the serenity of the family dinner table? You mention casually that your social studies teacher in junior high school calls himself a liberal, and you repeat some of the philosophy you have absorbed from him. If your father is a conservative, sparks fly. Perhaps some other admired adult figure is an agnostic. This sort of talk does not set too well at the dinner table if your parents are religious in an orthodox way.

Even though you may argue with your parents, express contempt for their notions and values, underneath it all you want your parents to stick by their guns. You have not yet developed your own selfhood, and you need a firm baseline, an anchor, a set of ideals—even though you may now be developing some questions about them—to bounce against. In this way you continue your quest for separation and independence. Your ideas about mother and father may be changing, but you don't want mother and father themselves to change. There are many confusing vistas in your new, confusing world; if these old stalwarts, these landmarks, also shifted, that would be too much.

If the parents do not hold firm and set an unchanging example, the adolescent suffers another loss. Such a situation will cause anger and guilt and result in depression.

You are, at this point, moving cautiously into change, new ideas, but you still continue to see things in black and white. You have high expectations of yourself and the world. This includes your parents, and you judge them with the same harshness with which you judge yourself.

It is par for the course at this point for the young teenager to feel that his parents have feet of clay, to question, even defy them—but only up to a point. What happens, however, to the adolescent who decides, rightly or wrongly, that his parents *really* have feet of clay? He can now see things he never did before. Perhaps his father cheats on his income tax. Perhaps his mother is a spendthrift. Perhaps both mother and father are prone to extramarital affairs. This really pulls the rug out from under the adolescent. Perhaps the parents are living together because of convenience, or social pressure, or for financial reasons, but they don't really like each other or, the adolescent feels, really belong together. When the parents appear as hypocrites in the eyes of the young adolescent, what happens to his secure base, his original set of ideas, all the things his parents taught him? At this point, the boy or girl can become very depressed and act out against the depression. Or he or she may feel a pervasive sense of shame; if the family is a zilch, then he or she is a zilch.

But what of the adolescent who is not able to separate from his parents, who remains dependent? This dependence reflects an unrealistic idealization of the parent, peculiar to a very young child. He relies on the strength and values of the parents and ignores their real defects. He decides that he can't really be as perfect as these people. This leads to frustration, disappointment, anger, and often depression or angry acting-out behavior.

The adolescent who progresses in a healthy way will find judgments becoming less harsh. The blacks become less black, and the whites less white. You will perceive life as a mature adult does, in various shadings of gray. You will become more tolerant of people. This is a direct result of your becoming more tolerant of yourself. You are unique, not a carbon copy, and it's okay. And so the arguments at the dinner table begin to quiet down, as you realize your parents are only human—not saints, not fools or villains—just human. Perhaps your father tends to be absentminded. At thirteen or fourteen, you'll think angrily, He forgot again! As you move toward maturity, you're more likely to think, Oh, that's the way Dad is. He must have been thinking about something else.

You begin to realize that you do not always have to approve completely of your parents' ideas and actions. Even more important, you begin to feel that they do not have to approve, in every detail, of what you think and do. You can begin to form a mutual nonaggression pact, which is the basis of civilized living.

You have proved yourself through experience, and have gained confidence as an individual, separate from anyone else. You are alike, but different, from your parents and everyone else. You have an ideal image of how you'd like to be, and you feel that you can reach this ideal. At the same time, your demands on yourself have also become less rigid and harsh. You are able to forgive yourself and others for shortcomings. You no longer have to feel so angry, and therefore so guilty, and possibly so depressed.

5/"A Great Big
Question Mark"

In the lyrics of a song by Kim Gannon, from *Seventeen*, a show popular some years ago, the young hero's parents lament their confusion over their offspring, calling him "a great big question mark."

You should realize, if you're somewhat at sea in this new world you find yourself in, that your parents are in a very similar boat. They are probably as confused and upset as you are.

How many times have you shrugged off your father's embrace, even though on some emotional level you wanted it? He probably doesn't realize that you can't endure the feeling of dependence that a couple of years ago you were quite comfortable with and, in fact, needed. He simply feels rejected. It's uncharted country he has entered, along with you, and he often feels that no matter which direction he takes, it's wrong.

The child who used to hang on his parents' every word, look on their opinions and pronouncements as gospel, now challenges all their values, their most cherished notions, and even criticizes their personal appearance and habits.

As you become increasingly verbal, increasingly adept at abstract thought, you become able to hold your own in an argument with your parents. Even if your argument is irrational, you can hold them off. Your parents have been around a long time and have had a lot of experience, but they're human. When they find their formerly docile child questioning them at every turn, and making a good case for his arguments, they sometimes begin to wonder about their own long-held ideas. Schools today are teaching much more sophisticated information than they did twenty to thirty years ago, and when kids use some of this information in discussions with parents who are not particularly well read, parents can become uneasy and even unsure of themselves as parents. They perceive their child's declaration of independence as a rejection of themselves. They may waffle, they may lose confidence in themselves. They, in turn, may even reject the child. For a teenager, it adds up to a loss, one of the reasons adolescent depression is epidemic.

Just as adolescents are experiencing losses, so are parents. For many years, the mother's primary responsibility has been meeting the needs of her family. Now a significant part of her family, her children, not only do not seem to need her any longer but make their independence of her quite clear. For mothers who have few if any interests outside the home this rejection can be devastating. It is especially crushing to mothers whose chief interest in life has been the children, to the relative exclusion of their husbands. These mothers can become very angry and re-taliatory toward the children. In some cases, they too feel guilty about their anger, and become depressed, with-drawing from their children at a time when the children need to feel consistent support. Even if a child is trying out his own wings, he still needs a home base, where he can count on affectionate respect.

The mother may well have special problems in relation to her daughter. She sees the girl growing into a dewy young female, while she herself searches the mirror for wrinkles. Her waist is thickening, her daughter's is slim. Some mothers become so threatened by these frightening comparisons right in their own homes that they may flip into wearing younger and younger clothing, using too much makeup, even flirting with the boys their daughters bring to the house. Or jealousy may result in unrealistic restrictions or unnecessary arguments. In instances such as this, a daughter sometimes becomes angry but feels helpless to change the situation. And such frustrated anger can lead to guilt and depression.

The father too experiences a loss during this period. He has always been the breadwinner, has been treated with respect. In most families, his judgment has been deferred to. Now his opinions are being questioned by children who previously accepted them completely. His personal-ity is attacked. Family discipline is being challenged. The little kid he taught to catch a ball and swing a bat now can catch and hit better than he can. Perhaps the kid is now taller than he is. He would shrink from a friendly wrestling match with this startlingly growing boy.

Just as the father is becoming increasingly uncomfortable with his son, he may be experiencing inner conflicts about his daughter. This little girl is blooming into an attractive young woman. He may have thoughts and feelings about her that he has always been taught are not permissible. At the conscious or unconscious level, he fears thoughts of incest. He is likely to withdraw from the girl-woman who now inhabits his house. He may even have an affair.

Some fathers handle these problems—in relation to both the boy and girl—by absenting themselves from the home. A father may stay at work longer. He may closet himself in his den or workshop—reading, working, watching television. He may spend more time on the golf course, with his sailboat, hunting or fishing. He may fight with or criticize the adolescents as a way of distancing himself from them.

The message this behavior may give to the girl is that she is unattractive to her father, and if this is the case, she must be unattractive as a woman—another loss. To the boy, his father's attitude may send a message that success means alienation, that if he is more successful than his role model—his father—he may be isolated.

Parents are often going through difficulties in their own right, aside from their relationships with their growing children. They are at a time of life when they are asking themselves where they are going and where they have been and are wondering if this is what it's all about. Women are facing menopause, which some see as a loss of femininity. Men are at a point in their careers where they often have to face the limitations that up to now they have kept hidden in a corner of their minds: They're not going to be presidents of their companies, or anything close to it. Young men are coming up, being promoted over them.

Just as adolescent children are experiencing a waxing of their potential, some parents during this period of their lives are experiencing a waning, a loss of dreams. This dichotomy within the family may create resentment, jealousy, rivalry, and tension between the two generations.

The adolescent's very freedom may be somewhat of a bitter pill for his parents. The father may have gone sour, stale on his job. But he can't quit. He has a family, a mortgage, a position in the community to support. He may feel trapped.

The mother also has responsibilities. She has to keep house, cook the meals, provide clean clothing. She feels the ultimate responsibility for binding the family together. She may feel she has been cheated out of a career, or if she has a career she may feel she cannot do it justice because of her commitments to her family.

Many parents, especially if they feel burdened by responsibility, may feel, in a passive or even active way, resentful of their children's freedom. Those kids really have it made, they think, they're living the happiest years of their lives. Oh yes, they have to go to school, but there's always an escape hatch. They can't be fired, for one thing. If they feel a little off when they get out of bed, they can get right back into bed and call it a day. Even if they do make mistakes, after all, they're just kids. This resentment of the child's relative freedom sometimes takes the form of the parents' viewing the adolescent as dependent, incompetent, and lacking in judgment. This can justify the adolescent's anger. It can erode his self-esteem, and hamper his ability to separate from the parents. All this can add up to depression.

There is another side to the parenting coin. There are some parents who had a childhood that was anything but happy, and many people like this are determined that their children will not have to go through what they did. They feel the child must have everything they themselves missed, not only material things, but freedom from responsibility. These parents put their children's wants and needs first and foremost. They themselves come second. They'll go without so the child can go to an expensive summer camp. The father will come home after a hard day at the office and mow the lawn, rather than cut into the boy's play time. He'll take the garbage out rather than ask the kid to do it. Mother will always do the dishes and never even ask her daughter to dry them.

This kind of parental behavior, no matter how well intentioned, doesn't work. It accomplishes exactly the opposite of what such parents are trying to do. The children are aware of what their parents are doing. They know their parents are sacrificing in order to give the kids everything, to make them happy. In a family like this, the kids can't work up the proper head of steam, the proper, natural anger that is necessary in order to separate from the parents. It would be too much to get mad at these pseudosaints, and the children are overwhelmed with guilt at their perfectly normal anger. This can plunge them into depression.

Sometimes parents, for one reason or another, may tend to rush their children, to push them into activities they are not ready for, are not interested in or comfortable with. Much of this sort of parent pressure takes the form of encouraging their children to socialize with members of the opposite sex. The mother who was not terribly popular during her high school years may feel a need to push her daughter into being a femme fatale. It may be that she wants the girl to have what she missed, or she may be trying to live *through* her daughter. This is the sort of parent who arranges boy-girl parties before most of the kids are ready for such heterosexual gatherings, who urges her thirteen-year-old daughter to date, to dress older, to do the things she really shouldn't be doing for two or three years.

Some fathers go into fits of anxiety if their sons do not exhibit the macho traits they feel a growing boy should be showing. They are terrified that they are going to have a homosexual on their hands. They push the boy into sports, whether or not he has two left feet. They want him to swagger and act tough—maybe smoke a little, drink a little. If the son has a male friend he seems overfond of, a father like this can be brought to the verge of a heart attack, certain that his son is on what he considers the unthinkable sexual path. Probably the kid is just too young to be interested in girls, or is still afraid of trying his luck with them.

The children of such parents may well feel something is

wrong with them. Few of these children can know that they are not wrong, that it's their parents who are wrong. They are too young to sort out who is right and who is wrong, but they certainly will give their parents the benefit of the doubt. Feeling that they themselves are at fault, convinced that they are not living up to their parents' expectations, they will develop a heavy load of guilt, with resulting depression.

Of course, parents had parents themselves, and they each had a different set of parents. Your parents may have been brought up quite differently from each other. Having had different models of parenthood, they may have sharply differing ideas of how to bring up their own children. The mother may be in favor of heavy discipline, the father of a lighter touch. The child quickly perceives that all is not solid on the parental front. Who is right? he wonders. How can he trust his parents' guidance when they have such different ideas? The mother may subtly or blatantly undermine the father's authority, or vice versa.

In recent decades a new breed of parent has come on the scene—the intellectual, the parent who reads books on how to bring up children. After World War II a spate of books and articles were published to the effect that children must be given wings, must not have their creativity curtailed, must be free to express themselves. These ideas certainly have merit, but many parents interpreted them as advice to raise their children without guidance or discipline. A couple of generations of people who had little or no restrictions as children has been the result. And, in spite of what the books say, this ultrafreedom does not make children feel happy. It makes them nervous, adrift, uninstructed, unguided. Therapists working with children who live in such homes have found that the children often feel their parents don't care enough for them to provide guidance, to set limits and boundaries of acceptable behavior.

Also in recent decades, a new type of family has become the norm. This is the nuclear family, as opposed to the extended family. Two or three generations ago most children had numerous aunts and uncles and first, second, and third cousins near by to bounce against. If the kid had problems with Mom or Dad, he could seek out a favorite aunt or uncle and talk things over. The nuclear home was not the be-all-and-end-all it tends to be today. The child had more alternatives in his relationships with adults.

Because of birth control, the state of the economy, women's increasing independence and interest in careers, as well as other factors, the family is getting smaller and smaller. This may have certain advantages for the children, particularly from a material, external point of view, but it also poses problems. The parents have more of their self-esteem, more of their ambition, wrapped up in a child when they have only one or two than when they have half a dozen. The child feels that more is expected of him.

As a result of this constantly shrinking nuclear family, family life has become more and more intense. Mistakes, or what are perceived as mistakes, loom larger. There are fewer escape hatches, fewer means of dilution of emotion, and everybody can get pretty nervous—angry, guilty, depressed.

The relative isolation of the modern small family can affect the parents as directly as the children. In the past, the parents had many adult relatives who were in the same parenting boat. These people had had the same kind of upbringing, held the same values. They could be a reliable source of support. They constantly assured one another that they were right. This sort of social circle of relatives has pretty much disappeared. Many American families move frequently today, and each set of parents tends to stand pretty much alone. Children tell about what their friends' parents are like, what they let their children do. This often undermines the parents' confidence, which subtly undermines their children's confidence. When this sort of situation develops, when the parents waffle, the child feels that his secure home base is becoming frighteningly shaky. The boundaries he needs are eroding; he begins to lose sight of the necessary limits against which to test himself. This can cause many of the emotional problems that are so characteristic of adolescence.

Another result of the relative isolation of the nuclear family is that some parents use their adolescents as confidants. This is often true in single-parent families or at times when parents are having marital problems. For an adolescent who is already overwhelmed by what he is experiencing, the feelings of helplessness, anger, and guilt are intensified.

What few parents realize is that the degree of violence of the child's revolt is directly connected with the amount of attachment he has to the parents. The anger and deval-

uation that he directs at the parents are part of this process of separation. For the child to move from being part
of the parents to becoming a separate person is a difficult,
emotionally wrenching process. In order to separate from
a situation—or from people, the parents—the adolescent
devaluates this situation, these people. If you can devalue
this setup that has been part of your life since birth, then
you no longer want to be part of it, which is exactly what
the adolescent is struggling with in his lunge toward
adulthood. A tug-of-war is a mutual activity, and this
loosening of the family tie is certainly a tug-of-war as the
child pulls in one direction—freedom—and the parents
pull in the other—maintenance of the interdependent
status quo. The degree to which the two sides tug is similar. If the child is closely attached, the parents are too,
and the struggle is all the more fierce.

So far, all we've been talking about is what is wrong
with parents—and of course they are less than perfect
because they had parents of their own who didn't do
everything perfectly. Few teenagers have parents who do
all their parenting so ineptly. Most, like the rest of us, do
some things well and other things badly. So, to strike a
balance, let's for the moment consider some beings who
probably don't exist—the perfect parents. What would
they be like? How would they relate to their adolescent
children?

First of all, they are content in themselves: they like
themselves. Their activities are a means of expressing
themselves, their interests and values. The mother may or
may not have a career. The father may be a raging success

or just another man in the street. They are not feeling angry or shortchanged in their lives. They not only like themselves, but they like and respect each other and are supportive of each other in the other's role and functions. They can respect and credit the other's differences and feel that what each has to offer is important. They stand together in the buffeting the adolescent is giving them. There is no negating or being contemptuous of the partner.

Their marriage is a model of interaction, of intimacy, that the child will emulate in his intimate relationships with others. The adult who is content in himself and in his marriage, who is fulfilled in his own life and relationship with his spouse, is more able to see the child as a separate human being, even from that child's earliest age. These exemplary adults are able to discern the needs of the child as separate from their own needs. They are able to move readily, and relatively comfortably, to bolster the child as needed. The child is secure in their love and respect.

In the child's adolescence they are able to judge the child's crises and needs. They are able to hold firm when such a stance is appropriate, to move back, to let go, when such action is helpful. As they see the child gain greater decision-making ability, they give him greater latitude. They give the child greater responsibility as the child is able to take it.

Because the parents enjoy being with each other, because they respect each other, because they are close, the child feels able to move away from them, to move toward the outside world, to other adult role models, to his peers, without going through paroxysms of guilt and self-recrimination. These perfect parents make it relatively easy for the child to move out, to move toward adulthood. Because the parents enjoy their lives separately from the child—because the child is not the dead center, the be-all-and-end-all of their lives—the child has permission to enjoy his own life, to become a separate person, to move into his own adult role. The child can enjoy his own happy moments, separate from the parents. He has permission to grow, on his own.

But even in this mythical model family, the adolescent is still going to revolt, to devalue, to be angry, to thrust his parents away. No one on this plane of human existence has ever seen a family in which the adolescent turmoil, questioning, stretching does not cause difficulty.

So, even under the best conditions, all this struggle you're going through is normal: it's part of growing up.

6/Changing Bodies

Nothing endures but change," said the Greek philosopher Heraclitus some 2,500 years ago. And change is certainly part of any period of life. But when you hit the age of twelve or so, the change becomes so rapid, so sweeping that it makes your head spin, your emotions reel.

At adolescence, our bodies, those uniquely personal clusters of protoplasm with which we so identify ourselves, seem to go out of control. We grow in all directions —upward, sideways, internally, externally. We look in the mirror and scarcely recognize ourselves. People who haven't seen us for a few months are startled. We can see the surprise in their eyes, and it's not always favorable surprise.

In any inquiry into the emotional problems of adolescence, we must take a close and extensive look at the physical changes.

The most important physical change in adolescence is the burgeoning of sex. It is these irresistible progressions in a child's sexual development that change him or her into a man or woman, that move him inevitably away from the family. As we have seen, it is this rupture in relationships with the parents that is one cause of much adolescent depression, growing out of the young person's anger and guilt.

Adolescence covers generally the period from ten to eighteen in girls and twelve to twenty in boys. In early adolescence, which may range from nine to fourteen in girls and ten to fifteen in boys, there are endocrinological and hormonal changes that may be so intense that the adolescent feels his body is out of control. This may spell the beginning of feelings of helplessness that he will carry with him throughout adolescence.

It is in the middle of adolescence that the sexual awakening really begins. Until this time, the individual has had sexual urges, but they were under control. They could be repressed, almost ignored. But now, in middle adolescence, sex really rears its often difficult head.

A child will inevitably direct his sexual impulses and fantasies at the adult of the opposite sex who is closest to him. In our family system, this means the mother for the boy, the father for the girl. As we saw, the child devises a method of living with these forbidden impulses. But now, in mid-adolescence, the demands of biology have become overwhelming. The adolescent's defenses against such desires, which have worked for as long as he can remember, are beginning to crumble. This is a very frightening thing. He or she is impelled to move abruptly away from these threatening love relationships by devaluing the parents, seeking shelter in anger, reaching out to substitute figures. This is the time when he moves almost completely into his peer group, and switches his adult heroes and heroines from his close, familiar parents to more or less distant objects of admiration: coaches, teachers, professional athletes, movie stars.

But even though the teenager is rarely alone, he still feels isolated, trapped in a new body filled with new emotions. He feels like a lone traveler—which does, to some extent, have its romantic aspect—but which even more is disquieting. He is more than ever before—and probably more than ever in the future—wrapped up in himself, and because of this he feels that the world is staring at him, judging him. And since none of us judge ourselves any too gently, he feels the world is not looking at him too kindly either.

If in his childhood something has gone askew—which is certainly par for the course in our less-than-perfect world —the adolescent moves into this new stage with built-in doubts about himself. Now, when being handed a new body by Mother Nature, he or she may look in the mirror and say, "Ugh, Mother, is that the best you can do? How about a little more height, stronger muscles, bigger breasts, slimmer legs?"

Most of us want to be like other people, but during adolescence the wish becomes an overwhelming drive. To be different means to be inferior. You can control the way you talk, the jargon you use, the clothes you wear, the opinions you express, but you can't control too much the way you look. If an individual feels he's out of sync with his peers in the way he looks and falls short physically of the All-American boy or girl ideal, there can be an emotional problem. It's very often part of this stage of life's journey. This can lead to a loss of self-esteem and increased self-consciousness.

In some cases, an adolescent will seek a role in which to hide. How many kids become class clowns because they're afraid people might laugh at them, so they become funnymen or -women so people will laugh *with* them? Another kid who feels he or she doesn't measure up physically may try to withdraw and become the class hermit who shuns extracurricular activities and whom almost nobody sees outside of school. Others may give up on attaining approval from their peers and try to get it from adults. They may become the teachers' pets, the kids who grind away at academic work to the exclusion of socializing and other activities, the kids who spend hours doing the dirty work of managing a team. They are all trying to run away from feelings of depression that come with not feeling accepted, feeling somehow different, feeling inferior.

The time period—mid-adolescence—during which the adolescent undergoes the most radical physical changes is not a long one, compared with the full life span of an individual. But it can seem very, very long to the adolescent stuck in the middle of it. It can seem interminable. Mid-adolescence generally ranges from about thirteen to sixteen for boys, and eleven to fourteen for girls. However, there is considerable variation among individuals. In boys, mid-adolescence can start as early as eleven and end as late as eighteen. In girls it can start as early as ten and end as late as sixteen.

These variations can be a cause of much uneasiness

among adolescents. Some boys go through much of their adolescence as short fellows, only to shoot up around the age of eighteen. But in the meantime they have seen other boys rising above them. They feel different, inferior. Some girls do not begin to menstruate until they are fifteen or even older, although most of the other girls have been menstruating for two, three, even four years. Some girls go through much of high school flat-chested.

Late bloomers such as these can often be victims of discrimination—by themselves and by those around them. They feel inferior within themselves, and their treatment by the group reinforces this feeling. The boys are looked down on by their taller friends. They can be handicapped in sports, at dances, and in general in their relationships with girls. The small, undeveloped girl is not granted full membership in the adolescent group, either by boys or by girls. She is looked on as a sort of little sister. She is excluded to some extent from the dating game by the boys and from the heart-to-heart womanly talks by the girls.

There are also the girls who develop breasts too early or—even worse, they feel—too fully. They are often self-conscious and uncomfortable, often try to shrink into themselves, to make themselves as inconspicuous as possible. Their feelings of self-esteem are damaged. Often the remarks of their contemporaries reinforce their feeling that something is wrong with them.

Although this time span is short in relation to an entire life, it is not so short in relation to the time the individual has already lived. At the age of twelve or thirteen, three or four years seems a very long time. When you're sitting in the middle of adolescence, it can be hard to realize that you are going to catch up, that you are going to become like the others in the long run. People may reassure you, but it's hard to believe, because it's something you haven't yet experienced.

Most boys measure their progress toward manhood by their height, their muscular development, the appearance of a beard and other bodily hair, the size of their sexual organs and ability to have an orgasm, broadening shoulders and deepening voice. Girls' criteria are the onset of menstruation and the development of breasts and hips. Deviations from the usual, from what the peer group considers normal, can cause the boy to question his virility and the girl to question her sexual adequacy. For these adolescents, the answers to who am I and where do I fit are universally negative.

There is a further catch to all this physicality, and that is, you're never quite sure how you look to the next person. Even the way you look at yourself is overlaid with emotional judgments. This is what psychologists mean when they speak of the "body image." The body image might not be the way the body really is. It is how it is viewed by oneself. It is a mental image, which may not be realistic for it goes beyond the actual physical facts and involves the emotional and psychological states one has experienced. How did you feel about yourself as a kid? How did other people feel about you? The body image represents not just the current but also the past feelings about the body. For the girl who has always wanted to be a boy, the burgeoning of the breasts can be most disquieting. It can mean the relinquishing of her fantasies. For the boy who has always been passive, these new demands that he be macho can be devastating.

The body image is only part of one's entire conception of oneself, but it is another aspect of this judgment of oneself that a person has to contend with, to come to terms with. It is a part of our sense of identity—either in a way that contributes to one's sense of self, or that detracts from it. And because adolescence is a time of such heightened questioning, such newness and insecurity, such critical observation of the self by oneself and by others, it is not surprising that the ordinary teenager inclines more to negative feelings about himself than positive ones.

Contributing to this negative conception of oneself is the ideal image the mid-adolescent has of what he would like to be. He has this personal fantasy along with the rest of humanity, and has as little likelihood of attaining it as everyone else has. But to the adolescent, the growing recognition that there is a gap between the ideal and the attainable, between imagination and reality, is something new. It is therefore much more of a shock to the adolescent than to older people, who have learned to soften their ego ideal so that it is attainable, who have come to terms with life. The later adolescent begins to move toward softening his demands on himself. He becomes more realistic, and therefore more comfortable with himself. The greater the distance between the adolescent's ideal image and his perception of himself, the greater the chance for depression.

Some adolescents' difficulties with their body images

are intensified by relationships within the family. Eileen's mother gave loud and clear messages that she was disappointed in her only daughter. At age forty-two, the mother still wore size 3 dresses, often boasted of buying sportswear in teen boutiques. To an objective observer, she appeared underweight and malnourished. Because Eileen was somewhat overweight, her mother refused to go clothes-shopping with her, saying she was "ashamed for Eileen."

Eileen's father, too, was very conscious of his body and of keeping fit. He jogged twice a day, watched his weight carefully.

At fourteen, Eileen was depressed and withdrawn. She turned her anger against herself. She hated her body. She began a fast that lasted thirty days, after which she was hospitalized. Her ideal body image had been very much influenced by her mother's perception of a body beautiful —even though her mother obviously had distortions in her perceptions of her own and her daughter's body images.

A large amount of anxiety-ridden questioning centers around the body's new sexual appetites. When a child's conscience develops in the Oedipal period, he tends to see things very much in a right or wrong, black or white context. When the sexual sap starts rising during adolescence, guilts and self-recriminations proliferate. Society has always laid down definite, more or less rigid proscriptions as to how people should handle their sexual drives. As people grow older, they may tend to deviate from society's strictures, or they may not, but at least they work out a modus vivendi—a way of living—for themselves. But the early and middle adolescent is stuck with the new, the unknown in this area, and he's also saddled with the feelings and ideas he acquired in his early childhood.

As the adolescent matures, his manner of thinking changes, his values are no longer so rigidly fixed, he is no longer so dependent on his parents. With these changes, he has a sense of himself as separate and unique. Now he is ready to move into intimate sexual relationships, neither losing himself in a relationship nor having to remain aloof to maintain his integrity.

7/One of the Crowd

When you're about twelve, and begin to move away from the parents who have supported and protected you all your life, you can feel somewhat shaky and qualm-ridden. You can't move into a vacuum: that would be just too intimidating, too frightening. Human beings are social animals, especially when they are young. They must have some footing in the social pile, some other person or persons to sustain them, for them to be with, to bounce off of intellectually, emotionally, socially.

When you are this age, in your search for a new style of relating closely, when you have turned away from your parents, you look for a friend—someone of your own sex and age, someone a lot like yourself—with similar interests and background. You may even look alike. You may call yourselves sisters or brothers.

You may be withholding information, refusing to share with your parents, but with your new friends confidence piles on confidence. You may endlessly discuss the plots of movies, talk about sex, trade opinions, give advice to each other, encourage each other in your new, expanding, formidable world. By doing these things, you are not only supporting your friend, you are in effect talking to yourself—confirming your own opinions, your own changing values. By finding acceptance from another person, you can more readily accept yourself. In this new, close relationship you find confirmation of your new self.

At this point in adolescence, boys pair up with boys and girls with girls. This is preparatory to moving out, in a year or two or three, into relationships with the opposite sex. When you are twelve or thirteen you feel much more comfortable with friends of your own sex, even though you may be eager, although not quite ready, for heterosexual relationships. But some parents worry about their children at this time. Sometimes—and this happens most often with boys, and with fathers—there is a fear on the parents' part that their child may be homosexual. They do not understand that this close attachment to someone of your own sex is an important stage in your development. If, the adolescent feels, someone very much like himself, someone who has heard all his inner misgivings, fears, and notions likes him, then he must be okay. He must be likeable, even lovable. This is the beginning of real acceptance of his new self.

Young children usually tend to be gregarious, to run with a group, but in early adolescence the group begins to take on a different meaning. Although the young adolescent usually has one close friend, he also is part of a larger group. And this group, unlike the kids' gangs of earlier years, is not just a collection of kids to play with. This

new, adolescent group is different. You are testing yourself in the group. You are working for recognition from
other members of the group. You are checking out the
reactions of others like yourself to yourself. You are not
only being judged in, and by, the group, but through discussions with your friends you are checking out new standards and principles, making new judgments about what
is right and what is wrong. If your own parents have im-
posed a 9 o'clock curfew on you, and other kids in the
group don't have to be home until 9:30, you go home to
your parents with ammunition. In fact, if your parents tell
you to be home at 9, but the others in your group don't
have to be home till half an hour later, you are likely to
get home at 9:30. You would rather risk the displeasure of
your parents than the derision of the kids. You are shifting
your need for support and commendation from the family,
from the adults in your life, to your peers.

In fact, you are very much taking on the code of the
group. You are worried about the possibility of being
estranged from the group. Far more important now than
any praise you may receive from your parents is what the
other kids think of you, for to be alone at this age can lead
to feelings of emptiness and depression.

This code of the group is something you carry with you,
whether or not you are with the group. Your responses,
particularly to adults, are in sync with the group code.
Often, when parents say they no longer know their child,
they're right. This new child is an amalgam of everyone in
his group. Even when alone with an adult, the adolescent
responds and reacts according to his group's code.

And so, although your parents may see you as rebellious, feisty, a closer look reveals the other side of the coin—your conformity with the group.

Teenagers tend to wear the same sneakers, the same blue jeans, the same hair styles. They have the same rock star heroes, dance the same dances, voice the same opinions. The teenage world is, and to some extent always has been, a cookie-cutter culture.

And yet, within this overall conformity, there are individual differences. In some ways adolescents are more innovative than adults. They invent their own dance steps; they often write poetry or compose their own songs. These are expressions of the individuality of the adolescent, even though he or she tries to look like all the other adolescents.

There is a saying that a supertidy desk indicates its owner has an untidy mind. He keeps his desk in ultraneat condition as a compensation; it makes him feel more comfortable with his whirling, undisciplined thoughts. The way an adolescent's mind works is somewhat similar. At this time of your life you are beseiged by rampaging sexual and aggressive urges. They are new, insistent; they cannot be ignored. They make you feel different from anyone else. You desperately seek a way to feel less different.

Since at this point you have made a declaration of independence from the family—what your parents have told you all your life you no longer accept as gospel—you very much need to belong to a group in which you do not feel different—or at least do not *look* different. This is your peer group.

The adolescent traditionally appears to the adults in his world to be out of control. And this is quite natural, for in a way you *are* out of control. You, yourself—more than anyone else—feel that you are out of control. You may be confused, a new person in a bewilderingly changing world. So it is very important for you to have a base of security. By being alike, you give one another support—there is strength in numbers. By being alike, you are also confirming this new person—you.

Your new aggressiveness and the anger that is natural to this period of your life can be very disquieting. But if other kids also are mad at their parents and the adult world in general, some of the guilt born from this anger is diluted. Many of your friends criticize their parents, their teachers, the way the previous generation has messed up the world. They support each other. In doing this they are implying to each other that well-known mutual encouragement—I'm okay, you're okay.

The support of the group gives permission to test and question parental rules, and adult rules in general. This support makes it easier to move away from your childhood need to obey blindly, to be a good boy or girl. You now start to check out some rules of your own—and sometimes come to see the validity of those your parents laid down. This process helps you move into making some judgments of your own, and to have more tolerance for yourself, which is an attitude you need for your changing life.

Just as you can't let yourself be different from the group, the group cannot tolerate any member who is

different from it. If you're not a jock, you're not in the
jocks' gang. If you don't smoke pot, you're not in with the
kids who do smoke it. Each high school tends to have an
elite, into which certain kids are accepted and others are
not. High schools have more rigid class structures than almost any other part of American society. When Sally began
acting out her anger in school by skipping school, cutting
classes, fighting, and smoking pot in the girls' room, she
ran into trouble with her friends, who were not into this
acting-out behavior. They didn't confront her. They just
talked around her when she was with them. They often
left her standing alone when they thought of something to
do, didn't call her at home, didn't invite her to be with
them. They ostracized her because she was expressing her
adolescent turmoil in very different ways than they.

When you enter college or the working world, you may
well look back on the set world of high school cliques and
in-groups and contrast it with the much more fluid and
tolerant world you have moved into.

The need to be accepted by the adolescent group leads
to the dares that boys and girls of this age may take from
their friends, the stream of minor exploits they may feel
they must perform. Taken to extremes, this need can lead
to vandalism and dangerous activities—walking a railroad
track when a train is coming, for instance, or taking drugs.

There is an added factor in your move away from your
parents into closeness with people outside the family.
That is admiration of an older person—either an adult or
an older adolescent. This is a person who will listen to
you, who will credit what you are saying, who is not hung

up on being an authority figure. This older person is, knowingly or unknowingly, imparting some of his own values to you. And in the process of considering new values you begin to realize that there are other values in the world than those of your particular parents. You begin to move away from your black and white judgments and what you have perceived as the black and white judgments of your parents. You are getting ready to change your mind on various things.

One of the most important areas in which an adolescent shifts his ideas is that of sex and affection. Heretofore, you have repressed sexual urges because of the dangers of closeness with people in your family resulting from the sexual taboos of our society. Now you are able to accept the idea of sex with a person who is close to you. You have begun to create a circle of closeness outside the family and are able to direct your sexual urges and fantasies outward, in a way society tells you is permissible, without fear and guilt. Sex and affection are merging; they no longer have to be kept separate, as they did when you were five. You can tolerate them as part of a whole.

At this point, the young adolescent transfers his or her feelings to the opposite sex, outside of the family. At first the boy views girls from a distance. He may show off, but he's not likely to take a girl to a movie or a dance. It is only as the boy strengthens his confidence in himself as a result of his relations with his own age-sex group that he is able to risk a relationship with a girl.

Girls become a boy's greatest joy, his greatest sorrow. He is drawn inexorably to them, but he is vulnerable and knows that he can't depend on them. Girls can be mean and critical; they can wither him with a word, with a glance. Worst of all, they can ignore him.

The changes in his body are confusing, often appalling. What do the girls think of his mask of acne? His growing limbs make him feel awkward. Is he tall enough? Will girls laugh if his voice, which recently dropped something like an octave, sometimes flips back to boy soprano? He has secret anxiety about the length of his penis and is embarrassed by unexpected erections.

No wonder he seeks safety in numbers. When he goes calling on a girl, he takes the gang along. Standing on the corner, he whistles boldly at passing girls, backed up by his buddies.

And of course, girls have problems of their own: menstruation, breast-development. They, too, are caught in that awkward moment between childhood and adult-hood. Ordinarily, the girl has had her main spurt of growth a couple of years earlier than the boy. She may be taller and heavier than he.

Girls, too, seek heterosexual acceptance and also have misgivings about their new bodies. They cling together, too, but for different reasons. They are not so much afraid of boys as envious of them, for in our culture—in spite of recent efforts at change—the male has the best of it. The girl hangs out with other girls in search of reinforcement of her own role. Being with other girls makes her feel more secure in, and confirms, her femininity.

Some girls, however, refuse to accept this submissive role. They are the tomboys—not the small tomboys who climb trees and jump across creeks, but adolescent girls who actively compete with boys: the star baseball player, the whiz at mathematics or science or some other course of study that our society considers more or less reserved for males. Girls such as this are influenced, as we all are, by the family constellation and have usually identified with a strong father or mother.

Adolescence can to some extent be easier for girls than for boys. In the boy's plunge toward manhood, he is being forced to shift his stance from dependency to protectiveness. He is very much afraid of being submissive, of being unmanned, and this colors his relationships with the opposite sex. He may see girls as threatening and aggressive.

This attitude of boys can be hard on girls. They are usually a couple of years ahead of boys in their development and are ready for one-to-one heterosexual relationships some time before boys are. Their more or less discreet overtures can be rather unnerving to boys, who are not ready yet for this sort of activity. The boy will often rebuff the girl, and to the girl this can be a blow to self-esteem, to her confidence in her developing womanhood.

There is no question that attitudes are changing in regard to male-female relationships, particularly concerning sexual intercourse. The majority of mid-adolescents, even though they may be involved in some sexual experimentation, stop short of intercourse. Often situations are arranged so that there is a built-in check. Double-dating is one method of this planned control, this mutual chaperoning. Parties, movies, parks—all are places where things can be started, but no one is likely to go all the way.

Other adolescents are catapulted into early sexual experience. Some are propelled by intense biological urges. Some act out of *counterphobia*, in which one does something one is very much afraid of, hoping to erase the fear. The macho man, for example, may be fearful of the passiveness, the normal femininity within him, and may act supertough to convince himself it isn't there, that he has nothing to be afraid of. The adolescent who is very frightened of his or her sexual urges may react by doing what he or she most fears, hoping that this may solve the problem. Some adolescents are propelled into sex by peer pressure. If they are in a group where sex has become the thing to do, they probably will go along; they don't want to be different.

Part of the pressure on adolescents today is caused by the changing mores of society. The roles of men and women—particularly women—are being rapidly altered. More and more, women are doing things that only men used to do. And to some extent, men are not so much afraid to express the feminine side of their natures as they once were. Thus it is natural that our sexual ideas and customs are undergoing rapid and confusing change. And this in itself can propel the adolescent into sexual intercourse sooner than his grandparents, or even parents. Most therapists feel that too-early sexual intercourse is not conducive to healthy emotional development. A mid-adolescent male, for instance, who has sexual intercourse when he is not yet at ease with girls, who sees them as dominant and dangerous, may become frozen in this emotional pattern. He may go through his entire life using sex to express aggression, rather than experiencing a more healthy mutual intimacy with his female sex partner.

After young people have accepted their own body images, understand how they fit into society, they no longer see the opposite sex as threatening; they are able to give credit to the opposite sex for its own special traits. When two young people *like* themselves, when they are certain of who they are, they don't have to lose themselves in a relationship. They can remain themselves. They don't have to be dominant or submissive. They know who they are. There is a mutuality of give and take. Two separate people can come together, but remain separate and unique, each liking his own uniqueness and respecting the uniqueness of the other. Premature intimacy can skew the entire settling of identity, your coming to terms with who you are. To wander around wondering who you are can be eroding to your self-esteem. It can lead to depression and even more serious psychiatric disturbances.

Marty has not completed the task of separation from his parents—particularly his mother. As a result, he has no firm sense of self. He waffles between being megalomanic —he knows more, is smarter, better equipped than anyone —and being resentful and jealous of others' successes. Underneath, he feels impotent and enraged because his ideal image and his perception of himself are so disparate. He feels there's something wrong with him. As a result, he can never be alone. He always has to have a girl friend with him. His resentment and jealousy of these girls takes the form of bullying. In an attempt to bolster his self-esteem he degrades them, insists that everything be done his way. But it doesn't work. Marty continues to feel there is something wrong with him, and he is depressed. Until he finishes the task of separation from his mother and establishes a firm sense of his own worth, he will not be able to establish a mature, satisfying intimate relationship.

Nature has catapulted you from one life to another—from one body, mind, and set of feelings to very new ones. Though patience is not a virtue popular with adolescents, you'd be wise to take one step at a time. Adolescence is a process, and to shortcut that process, to skip some of the necessary developments, will lead to problems that can last throughout one's life—to angers, guilts, and depressions that can become chronic.

8 / The Mind Grows, Too

A few years ago, when Jerry was ten, if he was cold he turned up the thermostat. The thermostat represented a simple, black and white fact to Jerry: I am cold. But now Jerry is sixteen, and that thermostat has hidden meanings, implications that he never dreamed of half a dozen years before.

Now he may think: How much oil am I using? How much is this costing my parents? Can they afford it?

Are there poor people who can't afford heat—perhaps old people or small children whose health, even lives, are in danger?

Is it right that the Mideast countries should charge so much for oil? Even in those countries, are all the people benefiting from the oil profits, or are just a few sheikhs piling up millions in their Swiss bank accounts?

Does the use of oil for heat really make sense? Are there other more efficient, more ecologically sound ways to produce heat—solar energy, nuclear energy?

Are American oil and financial interests profiting excessively by our need for oil? Are a few millionaires aiming to become billionaires? Are the politicians who run our country bought and sold, in the pockets of these moneyed interests?

All these thoughts can go flooding through Jerry's sixteen-year-old mind when he simply turns up a thermostat. Some of them are occasioned by the new, confusing world we live in. But part of Jerry's dilemma over turning up the thermostat is not peculiar to our special time: it is something that teenagers have always experienced as their intellectual capacities developed. As an adolescent you are no longer seeing things so simply, concretely, in black and white. An ability to think abstractly is changing your perception of your environment. You have been moving out into the world—intellectually—with a vengeance. In school, the courses you take introduce you daily to new aspects of the outside world. The television set at home has taken on new meanings, is sending out all kinds of new messages that you never noticed before. You no longer watch the kiddie cartoons. Now you are more likely to watch news shows, opinion shows, talk shows. You begin to notice that even the situation comedies have threads of the serious problems of life running through them.

All this information comes pouring in, and you are processing it, making deductions, asking: what if? You are now better able to judge a situation, to see both sides of an issue, than you were in the past. At sixteen, you are much more like an adult than a child in your reasoning. Intellectually, you have almost both feet in the adult world.

You no longer approve without question the standards of the adult world, the dictums of established society. You are no longer so satisfied with the tried and true. You are coming up with some answers of your own, as well as some questions of your own.

These changes separate you further from the adult world of your parents. This ability to think abstractly, to make connections, to see cause and effect, to be logical grows along with your idealism. You are beginning to know how you would like things to be, not just with the world but with your family. You are shocked when your parents get drunk and fight loudly in a restaurant. Your sense of decency is assaulted when you read about the local corrupt bank official. But even in less obvious ways you are confronted daily with adult versions of right and wrong. Your idealism has not yet been tempered by years of experience and the realities of "making it" in a real world. And so your idealism, buttressed by your new intellectual abilities, sets you apart from the pragmatic world of adults.

When one's physical, emotional, and intellectual aspects are changing so radically, one needs something to hang on to, some anchor, some inner place that is stable. In the past, even when you questioned adults' ideas, you still could use them as reference points. You may not have agreed with the old values, moralities, notions, but at least they were there, and in a way comforting. They were something to bounce off of.

What we have today is a whole new ballgame. So many values are crumbling that an adolescent finds it hard even to figure out what to question. The adults have got there first.

The atomic bomb that went off at Alamogordo is still reverberating. Will there be a world next year? Why worry about established structures when they can be blown away at the push of a button?

In our inflationary times, the adolescent sees his parents worrying about money as an element crucial to the whole family's life. They are no longer worried about little things; they are worried about critical issues. Can they afford to put meat on the table? Can they afford to run two cars, or even one? How on earth can they send the kids to college?

Problems lie not only in external, material forces, but in the psyches of the family members themselves. Divorce has become epidemic. And a sizable percentage of couples who don't get divorced wonder if they are right to stay together. The women's liberation movement has caused profound and rapid change. Mothers wonder if the direct route to fulfillment and happiness is really marriage and a family, as they were told when they were young. Now some say a woman is not fulfilled unless she gets a job, has a career, becomes her own person. How does a girl of sixteen know where to turn, which road to follow, whom to believe? The adolescent sees the family system in major transition, a situation unique in our recorded history.

This instability creates a special problem for you as an adolescent. Your emerging world is tenuous and uncertain in the natural order of things. And so, even though you want and need to question, you also need a measure of stability. If the world seems to be falling apart, if adults themselves are running scared, as is happening today, it can be pretty frightening for the adolescent to follow his own natural impulse to pull things apart.

Idealism has always been a factor in the psyche of the adolescent. Young people growing up are full of dreams of the way things should be. They have always been startled and dismayed, as well as confused, at the gap between the way things ought to be and the way they are. In the world of today, that gap has widened to a yawning chasm. Adolescents have always felt that adults have messed up the world, but today there is sweeping documentation that they have.

Hour by hour the electronic and print media bombard us with spectacular examples of a world gone wrong. Bad news sells, and good news is much less intriguing. The "Mother of the Year" story gets markedly less attention than the mother who drowned her children. Golden wedding anniversaries are relegated to a photo and a few lines on the social pages; the woman who shoots her husband makes page 1. The cop who beats up a kid gets plenty of notice in the press and on TV; the cop who patrols his beat and helps maintain responsible order can retire without a line.

All this sends loud and clear messages that violence is commonplace, a way of doing things. For an adolescent who is testing out how he fits into society, what is appropriate and what is inappropriate, how he can express his anger, these messages reinforce the tendency to act out. They weaken the prohibitions and restrictions of the conscience. This publicizing of violence might be *one* reason for the alarming increase in crimes against people and property that are committed by adolescents. This media bath that portrays the world as violent reinforces the adolescent's feelings of vulnerability and hopelessness.

The way we behave in Western civilization is far removed from the way we talk, and this is nothing new. You have picked up ideals of behavior all through your childhood, and have taken them quite seriously, whether you actually lived up to them or not. From the pulpit, at home, in school you were told the proper way to behave. If you joined the Boy Scouts you found out that a Scout is trustworthy, loyal, helpful, friendly, courteous, kind, obedient, cheerful, thrifty, brave, clean and reverent. But the signals you now receive from the world don't quite fit that well-scrubbed picture. You find that getting ahead, making money often involves less-than-praiseworthy behavior.

The chaos of the world can be rough on the intellectual processes as a young person grows up, for the adolescent is a seeker, and what you are seeking is yourself. You try this stance, that opinion, that role. By trying out different things in your new world, you constantly meet up with yourself. You constantly ask yourself why you did this, said that, espoused this opinion, got angry. You are searching, questioning, trying to find out who you are intellectually, where you are coming from, where you are at, where you are going. In wondering about yourself, giving yourself credit for your opinions, you are accepting responsibility for your uniqueness, your reality.

When you find that things in the adult world aren't

what they had seemed, aren't what you think they should be, the result can be acute confusion.

Another aspect of intellectual development as you reach mid-adolescence is the ability to contemplate the future and to place yourself there, by means of choices and decisions. But to plan and make choices, you must have a degree of predictability in your world and confidence that your choices and decisions will be viable in five or ten years.

More and more, people's behavior reflects the instability of the world. If things are so uncertain, some people—and not only young people—search for a stanchion, some fixed and secure point to cling to. Unable to tolerate uncertainty, they hold on to their childish patterns of thinking: black or white, no ifs, ands, or buts. Young people join cults and extremist political groups because they find that way of life comfortable. In these groups, the individual is expected to conform; there is no initiative; they live by the rules, with no questions asked. Right is right and wrong is wrong, and there is no in-between. Plunging oneself into a group like this represents to these people safety from a confusing and unstable world. I'm right, the cultist thinks; I've chosen the right side; I'm safe. This is one way for an adolescent to handle his feelings of helplessness when everything around him seems to be in such turmoil. He is freed from mature, abstract thinking; he has settled for the thought patterns of childhood, the concrete, right-or-wrong way of looking at things.

However, people who freeze themselves at this immature level of intellectual development pay a price, for they have tried to seal over their feelings of helplessness, of confusion, by following a leader or a code of hard-and-fast precepts. Underneath they still feel helpless and hopeless. The people of the cults, the religious extremists are usually depressed people, even though they sometimes present a smiling face to the outside world. Whether or not one goes so far as to get involved in such organizations, if a person is stuck at this level of intellectual development he is very likely to be depressed. The person who clings to this childish way of thinking has little self-esteem. His feelings of helplessness prevent him from thinking well of himself. This erosion of self-esteem causes anger, which he directs back against himself, making him a prey to depression.

There are other ways the adolescent might defend himself against these feelings of being afloat in a stormy, unpredictable sea. Some young people plunge into cynicism, the opposite extreme from fanaticism. They have been so disappointed by the world that they move radically away from the idealism of the growing adolescent. They sneer at everything, have no faith in anything, because they have no faith in themselves and in the possibility of having a meaningful life in the future. They have not been able to achieve intellectual growth and adopt a way of thinking that allows them to see the good and the bad, the complicated grays of life. They are still in a childish, black and white frame of mind, and they have chosen the black. They too feel helpless, hopeless, depressed. They may act out against this depression with acts of vandalism, destruction, *nihilism*—belief in nothing. This sort of adolescent may become the quintessential

dropout. He may do a job to get a paycheck, but he takes
no interest in his work. He may get himself onto the wel-
fare rolls, or get Social Security payments by feigning
mental illness. He may turn heavily to drugs or alcohol in
an attempt to run away from his depressed feelings.

Some young people who fail to take the intellectual and
emotional step into adulthood deal with their failure by
becoming pleasure-oriented. They live for the day and for
whatever turns them on. They back away from assuming
responsibility for the consequences of their own or others'
actions. They are always startled when their actions, to-
tally self-centered, upset other people. This is the kid who
will turn another kid on to pot, or coke, or whatever,
without a thought as to what it might mean to the other
kid. He just wants the pleasure and support of that person's company for the moment. When he is caught doing
whatever he is doing, he can never understand why everybody is so upset.

Achieving intellectual development in the teens is no
easy matter under any conditions, and many adolescents
get little help from the adults closest to them, their parents. Parents may actually inhibit their children from developing into mature, thinking people. In our society it is
so important to be popular, to be in step, that people who
do have ideas of their own are sometimes called kooks or
eggheads. Many parents, trained to be conventional themselves, give constant signals to the growing child that un-
popular, original ideas are *out* in that particular home.
Many, many young people get the message. They slav-
ishly follow the religions, the politics, the social and moral

notions of their parents. As various emotional problems are handed down in families from generation to generation, so often are modes of thinking.

Though this may not make for an interesting intellectual life as an adult, it does not necessarily result in depression. However, if the adolescent is in contact with peers who *are* moving into a more mature way of thinking, he may very well begin to question his own mental patterns. Will he look at things in the manner that was prevalent at home, or will he, to some extent, do his own thing? To some young people that can be a disturbing idea.

9/Mixed Messages

When you move into adolescence you find yourself in a whole new world of demands and pressures. These forces that come to bear on a teenager are not only new, they are much more intense than anything you've had to undergo during childhood. The protective blanket of childhood is fast falling away, and you may well feel naked and unprotected, a shorn lamb in a high wind. As a teenager you still do not have the privileges, the recognition, the rewards of adulthood, but some of the demands made on you certainly approximate those made of adults.

We live in one of the most sophisticated societies in history, a complicated world that demands a great deal of artfulness to survive in, to move through with any degree of success. The more sophisticated the society, the longer it takes to prepare its young people for full membership.

Two hundred years ago most young adolescents were working on their family's farms, or learning a trade from their fathers, or perhaps apprenticed to a journeyman artisan down the street, certainly not far away from the family hearth. The world then was much simpler, and moving into it was much simpler than it is today.

Even, say, a hundred years ago, when the industrial revolution had already been in full swing for several decades, life was simpler for the adolescent than it is now. At twelve or thirteen he assumed a relatively undemanding job in a factory, a store, or some sort of trade, while still living close to home.

Now, the adolescent must undergo training for almost his entire teen years. Child labor laws keep him from the simple—even if sometimes arduous—jobs of yesterday. The law says he must go to school until he is sixteen, whether he wants to or not. And society is so set up that the person who does not have what is considered a minimum education is doomed to menial work, very possibly for the rest of his life. This long training period our society has prescribed for its adolescents may well give you happier, more interesting lives as adults than people had in the past, but it certainly puts heavy pressure on you.

In the past, in fact from the beginning of recorded history, a boy followed in his father's footsteps. A girl learned to sew and cook and take care of a house and children. In modern society—particularly in America, which is indeed a land of opportunity—parents usually expect their boys, at least, to outstrip their fathers. Fifty years ago, when many fathers had only eighth-grade educations, boys and girls were expected by their parents to finish high school. In our day, a large percentage of parents who have a high school education want their children to get a college degree. And, of course, the day when the overwhelming percentage of girls expected to become housewives is past. Most girls today expect to do work that requires education and training, and a sizable percentage are aiming at full-scale professional careers.

As a modern teenager you find you are dependent for a good five years longer than in the past. Even though you are growing, taking on the physical and mental attributes of an adult, you are still trapped in a subordinate position. You are living in your parents' house, dependent on them for your food and shelter, and this proximity involves also an emotional dependence. Your parents continually remind you that you must do well in school, that you must measure up to what's expected of you. The message you are getting from them as an adolescent is: we will love you—*if*. This reinforces the feeling so many adolescents have: I'm no longer loved for myself; from here on it depends on what I do, what I accomplish, how I meet standards.

We live in a society that puts great emphasis on success, and this success is based on knowledge, experience, and reputation. Though you look more and more like an adult, and can often think like an adult, you have not yet gained the knowledge and experience that will bring you recognition as an adult. You begin to feel that what you do is not important, has no consequence—and this is very frustrating. When you are negated as a person—as you often are by adults—your feelings about yourself, your self-respect are eroded. If what you do and think are considered of little consequence, then *you* must be of little consequence. This is a strong factor in the prevalence of depression during the adolescent years.

The adolescent is a person in transition, and he is very much viewed that way by society. He is given little in the way of responsibility and productive work. An employer who must, by law, pay an adolescent the same as an adult for a low-level job, is much more likely to hire the adult over the adolescent because of the former's experience. Government programs have tended to put adolescents into make-work jobs, such as clearing brush or cleaning up river banks, a reflection of society's view that the adolescent is an ineffective, marginal person.

The area of sex, with its new physical pressures, has always been one of difficulty for adolescents. In the past, society clearly disapproved of a girl's having sexual intercourse before marriage. Now, however, society has changed its ways of looking at sex, and girls often find themselves in conflict between society's more permissive attitude and their parent's point of view. The result is great stress and often alienation from parents.

Sexual roles in our society have also been changing. A generation or two ago a boy knew what a man should be and a girl knew what a woman should be. No doubt about it. The male went out and brought home the bacon, often played ball in his youth, and avidly followed sports in his mature years. Depending on his dedication to the accepted masculine stereotype, he drank beer, ate pretzels, played poker, swore, and told off-color jokes—rarely in mixed company. The wife cooked, sewed, had babies, was responsible for the well-being of the home, was subservient to her husband—at least publicly—brought up the children, and probably went to church and did a bit of volunteer work on the side. Today most intelligent, active girls are looking forward to careers, often careers that would not have been open to them a generation ago. They engage in sports and activities that their mothers would have considered masculine. Boys and men are beginning to discover their feminine side; they are beginning to feel it is permissible to enjoy art and ballet, help with the children, do the dishes, cry.

There are masculine and feminine traits in all of us, and the modern world is beginning to realize this, and approve of people's expressing both sides of their natures. This may be, almost certainly is, a step forward in civilization, but it is also an occasion for further confusion in the already confusing life of the adolescent. The blacks and the whites have been washed into complicated grays, resulting in even more pressure on the teenager than in the past, and this is reflected in the growing prevalence of depression.

Another problem that faces many adolescents—particularly boys—is military life. Going into the service is bound to create tensions, if only because of the newness and unpredictability of the situation. It is certainly a new way of life for any civilian, and change causes stress. Aside from being drafted, people go into the service for a number of reasons, usually in search of security or job training. They may want to be told what to do and not really have to make their own decisions. On the other hand, they are told what to do very forcibly and rigidly, and there is little if any latitude for arguing. Authority makes some people more comfortable, but it can be nerveracking and offensive to others.

The codes of conduct in the service are often at some variance from the codes the young person has learned at home and in his own community. A military organization's ultimate purpose, after all, is to wage war when necessary. Many young people feel torn between what they have learned in church, school, and home and what they may be told to do by their military superiors. The entire concept of military force, used against another nation, has certainly come into question, particularly during the years of the Vietnam War. Many young people now tend to consider themselves more citizens of the world than of any particular geographic and political unit. Patriotism is not nearly so popular, especially with young people, as it used to be. It can conflict with the sort of idealism that many teenagers now subscribe to.

Even though one doesn't go into the service until age seventeen at the minimum, the shadow of the military hangs over younger adolescents. Even if no draft is in effect and no one is being forced into the service, that option is still there and every young person must take it into consideration. This is one more pressure society puts on its young members and it is one that can radically alter your life.

Another area of pressure for the adolescent is decisionmaking concerning courses. These decisions, beginning as far back as the seventh grade, can dictate the choices you will be able to make later. Deciding to take shop rather than Spanish, for instance, can determine the courses you will take in senior high school and whether or not you will go to college.

Adult decisions are being demanded of you. Of course, your parents influence these decisions to a greater or lesser degree, but you must still go along with these decisions. They become very much part of your life. You are being asked to make, or at least participate in, adult decisions without the benefit of much life experience. Yet, in general, the adult world still looks on you as a child. As an adolescent you often feel you are getting mixed messages —you're a child but not a child, a young adult but not a young adult—and this is just a part of the pattern of confusion that is so characteristic of life as an adolescent.

Mixed messages are very much a part of the modern adolescent's life. Since World War II we have lived in what has been called a child-centered world. Because families are now usually made up of fewer children—one or two, compared with the large families of the past—parents brood about their children more. They have a stronger emotional investment in each child. In many families, everything revolves around the children. No arduous demands are made of them. The boy is not expected to do meaningful work, such as keeping a garden, or contributing in any way toward the family income. The girl is not expected to help with a brood of younger children. This American way tends in infantilize the child, right up through adolescence.

But when the child moves into his teens, the outside world *does* make demands on him, in no uncertain manner. His teachers expect him to produce, almost to the extent that an adult must produce at work.

Thus, on the one hand, you are often treated as a child at home, and this continuing dependence can create a sense of inadequacy; yet outside the home you know that you must shape up and produce. The messages are indeed mixed.

10/This Rocky Trip

What does it all amount to, this rocky trip through the teenage years?

The goal is to prepare yourself for adulthood. You are gearing up to take your place as a mature member of adult society. You are aiming to prove yourself sexually, socially, economically. You are getting ready for marriage or for some sort of intimate relationship with another person. You are getting ready to support yourself, to find your place in work. You are casting about for a creative role to perform in the community, becoming aware of what is going on around you in society, preparing to take some part in it.

You must find a balance between the sexual, the social, and the working person—between love, play, and work. There is a theory that a person's energy is similar to a closed circuit, that everyone has just so much energy. If energy and interests are highly invested in one area, the person who wishes to maintain an equilibrium—a *homeo-stasis*—must withdraw energies in order to place them in other areas.

Do you know a successful business or professional man or woman whose only interest is in success? Who works all day, evenings, weekends? Who cannot leave this work to take a vacation? These are emotional cripples who may be successful, but who have sacrificed their intimate relationships and their pleasure in leisure activities; love and play are lacking. Many of these people are candidates for mid-life crises—and depression.

Adolescence is the period during which you find out who you are, where you fit in with your peers and with society. It is a period during which you recognize your similarities to others and your differences from them. You are unique. There is no other person with your history, your feelings, your interests, your personality, your identical physical characteristics, your strengths and weaknesses.

When you have arrived at a sense of self—your identification as a man/woman, a worker, a lover, a friend—and can find satisfaction in these areas, you are mature. You have achieved an ego identity—you know who you are, and you like who you are. This is apparent to others because you act consistently in a way unique to you that permits others to know how you will behave and react. It is the skewing of these parts of yourself, a lack of balance, which leads to depression and other psychiatric illnesses.

The main thrust of your struggle during adolescence is emancipation from your parents. You have to leave the nest, the safe home, and move out into the world on your own. Breaking this tie with the people who have been closest to you since you were born, your parents, is no easy matter. You must come to realize how you want to be different from your parents, and also how you want to be like them. No mature person can be a carbon copy of another, and young people who do not come to terms with their own uniqueness limp through life in a very mixed-up way. These are the women who even though they have their own family call Mama every day for advice and comfort; they are the men who stop in at their parents' home on the way to their own homes every night to report to Mom and Dad, much as they did as young children. They constantly look to other people to take care of them or give them advice. There are many ways in which this failure to gain independence—and maturity—can manifest itself. These are the boy-men and the girl-women of our society, and they are legion.

This emancipation is propelled by the adolescent upsurge in your sexual and aggressive feelings. It is abetted by your physical growth, for now you are actually looking down on, rather than up at, many of the adults in your world. With this sudden, startling change in size and strength, your whole perspective on those around you begins to change. And their perceptions of you must change, too. It's hard for parents to cuddle a fourteen year old the way they did a nine year old.

This emancipation is also aided by the development of the intellect. You are now able to think abstractly and logically, the way an adult does. You are able to contemplate the future. You can do deductive thinking, find reasons why things are happening.

This emancipation is reinforced by your move away

from your parents to your own age group. Also, for the first time you find other adults who become important to you as role models, heroes, someone to pattern yourself after.

But this emancipation also entails a loss. It's a loss of the unconditional love you received as a child. You must change from a passive receiver of love to a person who is responsible for people's reactions to you. You must give up your status of complete dependence on your parents, and move into a role of independence, of being a separate person.

The way in which you respond to these losses will determine whether or not you will be depressed.

There is a theory that prolonged stress leads to feelings of helplessness. The way you respond to these feelings of helplessness determines whether these feelings will escalate into depression. As an adolescent you are certainly under prolonged stress. All the changes we have been talking about are prolonged and stressful. And this possibly, according to some theories, can cause biological changes that result in depression. A body under stress uses nutrients at an increased rate. These nutrients, according to proponents of this biological theory, are needed by the central nervous system to manufacture biogenic amines, which reduce the danger of depression.

There are not only stresses on the adolescent caused by changes in himself, there are external stresses. Maybe you are in some way isolated from your peers, unable to participate in sports and other forms of exercise. This lack of sensory and motor stimulation, this lack of opportunity to discharge energies and build your body, can be a source of stress—and depression. Maybe you are in a situation where you have little intellectual stimulation; you may be taking a course that doesn't stretch your mind, or you may find yourself in a social milieu not up to your mental capability. Perhaps you can't depend on people you should be able to depend on; your parents may be divorced and you seldom see one of them, or they may simply not be supportive people. Maybe you can't find people outside your family who are congenial, who are like you, and who like you. In the swirling, confusing world we live in, many of us tend to emphasize our own needs, to the relative exclusion of concern for the needs of others. This "me-ism" contributes to the unpredictability of life today and causes the developing adolescent to feel even more deprived and, as a result, hopeless. It's hard for a young person today to make sense of his experiences. All of this adds up to the likelihood of adolescence being a prime time for depression.

Unhappiness and anxiety in adolescence are not always bad; they can stimulate the adolescent to change, to re-work and reorganize his personality to fit into society. In fact, the ability to feel sad, unhappy, and anxious is a prerequisite to mature emotional development. It is not the normal kind of unhappiness and anxiety but severe pressures and stresses that can lead to self-recrimination and depression. In the next chapter we'll discuss ways in which you can keep these normal sadnesses from escalating into a full-blown depression.

11 / Keeping Depression from Escalating

Depressed moods *can* escalate to full-blown depressions.

Feelings of being let down, sadness, pain because of a threat to one's sense of well-being, and fear of not being able to live up to one's expectations are normal and natural reactions to the vicissitudes of life. To have feelings of sadness, and to acknowledge your own and other people's limitations are signs that you are functioning on a mature emotional level.

However, you must be alert against allowing these "soft spots" in your ego to take over. All of us tend to see the world through distorted glasses of one sort and degree or another. If a girl has decided she is not pretty, she will read rejection into the most casual of contacts she has with the opposite sex, even when no such rejections were intended. If a person feels he is unlikeable, everyone's actions, tones of voice, comments will reinforce that judgment the person already has made of himself.

We know that depression can be a result of an unhealthy reaction to stress and loss. When you undergo such stresses and losses, it is natural to be worried, sad, rather pessimistic. It is natural for you to withdraw somewhat from the world around you.

But—if you continue in this negative frame of mind, if you see the world in this distorted fashion, you begin to feel that you have no power to change the situation. You begin to feel that you're locked in. You begin to feel helpless, hopeless, anxious, woeful. You may be preoccupied with your body, have difficulty doing what you're supposed to do; you may give up easily. You may find yourself too dependent on others, constantly asking advice, being overcompliant.

This can lead to total demoralization. You may be filled with self-recrimination. You may be prone to self-destructive behavior. You may become nihilistic—not care about anything. You are in despair.

A really depressed person just sits. He or she is unable to function. The sense of reality is impaired. The slightest problem seems overwhelming. Bodily processes are often slowed down or altered. Sleep patterns are disturbed; the person may have nightmares. He has no sex drive, may be unable to eat. A girl's menstrual cycle may be abnormal.

How do you prevent things from getting this bad?

First of all, since depression is a result of unexpressed, *unrecognized* anger, it's important to recognize your anger. It's healthier to know that you're angry, and to feel it, than to be depressed. So, first recognize and accept your angry feelings.

Since you can't go around destroying things or beating people up, physically or verbally, a good way to get rid of your anger is to work it off.

Some therapists will tell you to scrub a wall or chop wood, to do hard, arduous work. This is one way to dissipate the anger. It also helps you feel better about yourself because you've accomplished something. It is also a way of punishing yourself, and punishing yourself alleviates the guilt you feel for being angry.

Depressed people tend to see everything in a very personalized kind of way. If her boyfriend doesn't call one night, it's because he never wants to see her again, because she's unattractive. If he gets a D in chemistry, it's because he's stupid and will never amount to anything. How do you offset this distorted view of events so that you don't get caught up in depression?

Use your logic. Make a conscious effort to put things into perspective, see them differently from the way you are temporarily seeing them through your deep-blue spectacles. It's especially important to put your disappointments in perspective.

It might help to make a list of things that have been good in your past life, of activities you've enjoyed or been good at in the past, of things you enjoy or are good at today, and activities that you might look forward to. Make it a point to try one of these activities.

Check out your assumptions about yourself and others. Do you have to be perfect, or a total failure? Isn't there a middle ground? Must you do this or that in order to be acceptable at all times, or can you be yourself?

When we're depressed, we tend to blame other people. Bill didn't smile at me; Betty passed me in the hall without a glance. Adolescents particularly tend to lay a heavy load of blame at the door of their parents. Many of these slights and woes that a depressed person perceives are wholly imaginary. A person who is depressed *expects* such putdowns and tends to create them even though they are not there in reality. If you are depressed you should be careful to see the people around you correctly. Try to put yourself in their places. Perhaps Betty and Bill just didn't see you. Perhaps they were preoccupied with problems of their own. To keep a down mood from ballooning into a depression, it's a good idea consciously to try to keep things in perspective.

What are your goals? Are they realistic? Can you achieve them? Or are they so high that your world is full of "shoulds?" "I should be this," "I should do that." Do something that you know you're good at, that you know you'll enjoy. This will give you a sense of accomplishment, with a resulting sense of pride in yourself. Furthermore, it will encourage you to set goals you can reach now, and this will mitigate feelings of failure.

Maintain a regular routine. This will help you feel more in control of your environment. Eat when you're accustomed to eating. Get up at a regular time.

Get some exercise. This can go a long way toward lifting blue moods. During the exercise you will have a respite from your depressed feelings, and you're likely to feel better afterward too, for both physiological and psychological reasons.

Talk to friends, and tell them how you feel. This will help you feel less isolated. Isolation increases your feelings of helplessness and hopelessness.

Stay away from other depressed people. Depression can be contagious.

Keep a journal or diary. This is a good way to get rid of feelings that are trapped inside you. Putting things down on paper can help you sort things out, to see things in perspective.

These are all ways of warding off feelings of hopelessness and helplessness. You may find some of them of more value than others to you, depending on where you are emotionally. Each of you has to find your own way.

Most important—realize that being sad, unhappy, blue during the teenage years is normal. It is transitory. If you understand the stresses and losses, the trials and tribulations that all adolescents necessarily go through, you have made a giant step toward warding off depression.

12/Danger Signals—
And Where You Can Get Help

There is no question that depression in adolescents is widespread. Current figures show that suicide is the third leading cause of death in people between fifteen and twenty-four in the United States. Only accidents and homicides precede it. But many seeming accidents—and young people have a high accident rate—can really be covers for suicide.

For people between ten and fourteen, suicides have risen 32 percent since 1968. These figures don't include self-destructive behavior, which takes the form of drug and alcohol abuse, criminal activity, and excessive promiscuity. "Blowing your mind," "knocking yourself out," "getting dead drunk" are suicide equivalents. This sort of behavior is an attempt to block out the chronic anxiety underlying the loneliness, helplessness, and hopelessness of a depression. And it doesn't work because you always come back to you—your anxiety, your loneliness, your hopelessness.

What are the danger signals? When is it time for you to become worried, to look for help? What are the signs that you are moving beyond the unhappy, sad, or anxious feelings that are part of life to an enveloping depression?

Therapists look for certain signs when they are trying to assess the degree of depression in a young person.

An obvious sign is isolating yourself for long periods of time.

Another sign is a change in your sleeping pattern. Do you have trouble getting to sleep at night? Do you wake up during the night with a feeling of dread and have trouble getting back to sleep? Do you wake up early in the morning, still tired, but unable to go back to sleep? You can be spending a lot of time in bed—which is part of the isolation syndrome—but still drag around exhausted most of the time.

Do you have trouble concentrating? Do you read a page and find that you're unaware of what you have read? Do you find it difficult, or nearly impossible, to function? Are you a person who wants to be a writer, perhaps, who was outstanding in this area when younger, but who in adolescence finds it impossible to get words down on paper? Are you interested in mathematics, aiming at an engineering or other scientific career, but now find it difficult to juggle the necessary abstract figures and concepts in your mind?

Do you find that you're not interested in anything, for long periods of time?

Do you feel you just don't want to try anymore? Do you have constant, recurring thoughts of suicide? Just about everyone at one time or another toys with bidding this cruel world goodbye, and perhaps luxuriates in fantasies of how people will storm the funeral home wailing regrets about the fine person who's departed, who should have been treated better. These are normal fantasies. But if suicide is often on your mind, seriously, it can be a real danger sign.

Do you feel you're not much use to yourself or anyone else? Are you hopeless, and do you feel helpless to do anything about it? Do you despair of anything changing for the better?

Suicide attempts are always serious even though the person may not really want to kill himself. Attempts of this nature are basically a cry for help, a cry for someone to take notice, to help the person do something about his depression. But many of these suicide attempts do succeed.

Another danger sign is pervasive, continuous feelings of shame, guilt, blame, disappointment, rage, helplessness, and hopelessness.

Do you indulge in self-destructive behavior such as drug and alcohol abuse, antisocial behavior such as criminal activity, vandalism, excessive promiscuity?

Are you consistently preoccupied with physical symptoms? This can also be an indication of an underlying depression.

Long-term depression is probably one of the most debilitating, hurtful feelings a person can have. No one should have to suffer from it.

One of the ways to ward off depression as an adolescent, of course, is to understand the turmoil, the changes, the challenges of this time of life. It's therapeutic simply to understand the whys of your down feelings and to know you're far from alone in having them.

If your depression is hanging on and on, however, you should seek outside help as soon as you recognize the danger signals. Many people have great difficulty in approaching a counselor or psychotherapist. They think that doing this indicates weakness. It is helpful to keep in mind that it takes greater strength to go looking for help than it does to shrink into oneself and do nothing. Someone who is depressed finds it especially hard to reach out.

Where should you start looking for such help?

Many clergymen now are trained in psychotherapy, and even if your clergyman is not so trained he probably will be able to direct you to qualified help.

Doctors and school counselors are also good sources. They can steer you to qualified therapists.

Many communities have hot lines, places that you can call anonymously. The people manning these phones will talk to you—it helps just to get some of these things off your chest—and the hot line volunteers also can tell you where to look if you need professional assistance.

The yellow pages of your phone book list social service agencies, mental health facilities, family and children's agencies, psychiatrists, psychologists, and social workers. Almost all of these professionals will see an adolescent at least once without requiring parental permission. If therapy is to continue and the professional requires parental permission, he will not share what you tell him with anyone, including parents, unless you approve.

If the professional therapist sees that there are external factors in your life that are causing undue stress—such as situations at home or in school—he may, with your permission, involve the people who are causing the stress in the attempt to resolve the difficulty. For example, sometimes a therapist will find that a depressed adolescent is reacting to the marital problems of his parents. In cases like this, family therapy, involving the parents, may be indicated. The problem is the parents' more than the adolescent's.

In recent years, rap centers have been established for adolescents throughout the country. These are places where you can just walk in, without your parents' knowing, and join therapy groups with your peers, or have individual counseling.

To sum up, you are not alone. If you are depressed, there is help waiting for you, and you can help yourself. Nothing in life is permanent. Depression can be licked, and you can do it!

For Further Reading

Nonfiction

Bernard, Jessie. *The Future of Marriage.* New York: World, 1972. *New forms marriage is likely to take.*

Caplan, Gerald, and Lebovici, Serge, eds. *Adolescence: Psychosocial Perspectives.* New York: Basic Books, 1969. *Directed to child psychiatry professionals, this book has several sections that can be of interest and value to adolescents.*

Dowling, Colette. *The Cinderella Complex.* New York: Simon & Schuster, 1981. *Do women really want to succeed professionally, or do they prefer to be taken care of?*

Fine, Louis. *After All We've Done for Them.* Englewood Cliffs, New Jersey: Prentice-Hall, 1977. *Written from the parents' point of view but interesting from the other side of the fence as well.*

Friday, Nancy. *My Mother/My Self.* New York: Delacorte, 1977. *Complexities that pervade the mother/daughter relationship.*

Gordon, Sol. *You.* New York: Times Books, 1975. *Enhancing life in the areas of friendship, school, work, home, etc.*

Langone, John. *Bombed, Buzzed, Smashed, or . . . Sober.* Boston: Little Brown, 1976. *The problem of drinking as it applies to teenagers.*

Langone, John. *Like, Love, Lust: A View of Sex and Sexuality.* Boston: Little Brown, 1980.

Nolan, Edward. *How to Leave Home and Make Everybody Like It.* New York: Dodd, Mead, 1977. *Practical suggestions for achieving independence.*

Paine, Robert. *We Never Had Any Trouble Before.* Briarcliff Manor, New York: Stein & Day, 1975. *Described as "A Handbook for Parents" on such subjects as appearance, drugs, sex, living together, and suicide, this is also interesting from the teenagers' point of view.*

Richards, Arlene and Willis, Irene. *How To Get It Together When Your Parents Are Coming Apart.* New York: David McKay Co., 1976. *The title tells the story.*

Rubin, Zick. *Liking and Loving.* New York: Holt, Rinehart & Winston, 1973. *How and why people relate to one another.*

Scarf, Maggie. *Unfinished Business.* New York: Doubleday, 1980. *Depressed women at various stages of life.*

Sheehy, Gail. *Passages.* New York: Dutton, 1976. *An interpretation of life patterns through personal anecdotes and psychological insights.*

Toffler, Alvin. *Future Shock.* New York: Random House, 1970. *An overview of our rapidly changing world and the choices confronting us.*

Fiction

Bauer, Marion D. *Tangled Butterfly.* New York: Clarion/Houghton, 1980. *A 17-year-old girl contemplates suicide.*

Bradford, Angier, and Corcoran, Barbara. *Ask For Love and They Give You Rice Pudding.* Boston: Houghton Mifflin, 1970. *A boy, isolated from his parents, seeks his identity.*

Greenberg, Joanne (Green). *I Never Promised You A Rose Garden.* New York: Holt, Rinehart & Winston, 1964. *An autobiographical novel about a schizophrenic girl.*

Greene, Shep. *The Boy Who Drank Too Much.* New York: Viking,

1979. *A young hockey player, unable to meet his father's expectations, turns to alcohol.*

Guest, Judith. *Ordinary People.* New York: Viking, 1976. *The mental breakdown of a boy whose mother turns against him after the death of his older brother, her favorite.*

Josephs, Rebecca. *Early Disorder.* New York: Farrar, Straus & Giroux, 1980. *Suffering from anorexia nervosa, a girl reaches the verge of starvation.*

Van Leeuwen, Jean. *Seems Like This Road Goes On Forever.* New York: Dial, 1979. *A girl regains a grasp on reality through a better understanding of her domineering parents.*

Index

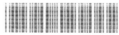
DATE DUE			
DEC 23			
JAN 25			
MAR 18			
DEC 12			
DEC 10			

**616.85
MYE**

Myers, Irma.

Why you feel down--&
what you can do
about it.